VEDIQUANT

Abha Sharma is an author of five books with Rupa Publications, India, including the novel *The Night of Fear* and motivational books in The Making of the Greatest series. As a qualified university-level educator, she has worked extensively with international industry leaders in online education and with prestigious higher education institutions. As a life-skills coach, she has followed her passion of helping individuals think beyond the ordinary. The intriguing mysteries of existence have been the driving force behind her study of various disciplines, including biology, literature, quantum physics and spiritual philosophy. This book is a result of years of scientific learning and deep curiosity along with personal experiences bordering on mysticism. You can learn more about her through her LinkedIn.

VEDIQUANT

Vedantic Truth in Quantum Science

Abha Sharma

RUPA

Published by
Rupa Publications India Pvt. Ltd 2023
7/16, Ansari Road, Daryaganj
New Delhi 110002

Sales centres:
Bengaluru Chennai Hyderabad
Jaipur Kathmandu Kolkata
Mumbai Prayagraj

Copyright © Abha Sharma 2023

The views and opinions expressed in this book are the author's own and
the facts are as reported by her which have been verified to the extent possible,
and the publishers are not in any way liable for the same.

All rights reserved.

No part of this publication may be reproduced, transmitted,
or stored in a retrieval system, in any form or by any means,
electronic, mechanical, photocopying, recording or otherwise,
without the prior permission of the publisher.

P-ISBN: 978-93-5702-823-3
E-ISBN: 978-93-5702-943-8

First impression 2023

10 9 8 7 6 5 4 3 2 1

The moral right of the author has been asserted.

Printed in India

This book is sold subject to the condition that it shall not, by way
of trade or otherwise, be lent, resold, hired out, or otherwise circulated,
without the publisher's prior consent, in any form of binding or
cover other than that in which it is published.

Contents

Note to the Reader vii

1. The Mysteries 1
2. Mysteries Deepen 15
3. One Reality—*Ekam Sad* 33
4. Is Everything as It Appears to Be? 50
5. Spooky Actions 63
6. Cosmic Vibration Only—*Chitta Spanditam Eva* 78
7. The Mysteries of Space and Time 87
8. Is the Real Unreal? 106
9. Death and Immortality 123
10. Transcending Unknowability 136

Acknowledgements 151

Note to the Reader

This book is an attempt to grasp the beauty of the perpetual human quest—the quest of the true nature of our existence. It aims to approach complicated concepts of Vedanta and quantum science through the curiosity of a student, a lay observer, and not of the expert. The purpose is to simplify the concepts for readers yet uninitiated into either of the disciplines. This book is an attempt to present the deepest mysteries and secrets of Vedanta and quantum physics in a simple and easy to understand form.

The two disciplines are widely different, but also turn out to be inadvertently echoing each other. This is because the two have a shared goal—the quest for the ultimate truth of the universe. The intent is to celebrate the similarity in these two widely different approaches, not to claim that the two are merely mirror images of each other. Just because the destination is the same does not mean that the two paths are copies of each other. The subject needs to be studied from the unique perspective of 'Vediquant', a fresh and unbiased approach towards the parallels between Vedanta and quantum science that celebrates their similarities without claiming their influence on each other.

The book does not, in any way, support or propagate pseudoscience that operates on an arbitrary linking of quantum science with spirituality. Unfortunately, a fragmentary understanding of quantum processes often leads to unsubstantial claims about their effects on healing, wellness, etc—something that the book distances itself from.

This book is also not a commentary on any aspect of religion. It does not in any way seek to establish any sort of hierarchy or undiscovered connection between Vedantic philosophy and the development of quantum science. Anecdotes of famous physicists' fascination with the Upanishads are well known, and quite expected too, because any seeker of truth would naturally be drawn to any wonderful medium that helps them approach it. The same holds true when modern Vedantic scholars often quote from quantum science. The Vediquant approach, therefore, is essential in this environment, to rein in the temptation of comparing one discipline with the other, and to smoothly combine the ideas of both to reach the truth.

Vedanta and quantum science are two extraordinary attempts at understanding the true nature of reality. They are widely divergent paths to the same goal. The book attempts to respectfully understand each approach and to draw attention to the commonalities. Since the goal is the same, there are bound to be agreements along the way. Welcome to the exciting journey of magical revelations!

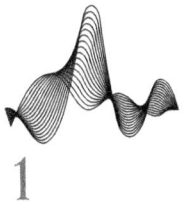

1

The Mysteries

On a warm spring evening, a 20-year-old college student on a photography assignment with his group, stood on the sands of a desert, gazing at the darkening skies. The location, far removed from any trace of civilization, was extraordinary—the horizon in the far distance seemed to levitate with the radiating heat. He sat down on the ground and leaned back. A sweeping panoramic glance in the range of his vision gave that breathtaking feeling of being located inside a giant sphere. As the blue sky smoothly transformed into the deep black of the moonless night, tiny dots of shining stars materialized on it and swiftly increased in number. Wherever he looked, stars appeared as if his eyes were painting them. Soon, the black sky was a canvas on which were printed cosmic patterns. Tears spontaneously rolled down his face. He was mesmerized, overawed with the timeless grandiosity that he was witnessing.

∽

Vediquant

With no interest in spirituality or astronomy, what was it that had overwhelmed him?

The feeling of awe is shared by scientists and philosophers trying to crack the workings of the world—from figuring out the incredibly fast energy transfer in human cells to finding out what constitutes the invisible dark matter. As a 16-year-old, Albert Einstein mentally chased light beams, trying to figure out what it would be like if he was moving at the speed of light. The nature of time has unnerved innumerable minds—what if the past, present and future coexist?

There are questions that have haunted humankind through decades, centuries and millennia, irrespective of cultural, geographical and technological differences. Centuries have passed and the world has changed unrecognizably since the time humans first appeared on this planet. We evolved and created the most sophisticated civilizations. As we developed better methods of exploring reality, incredible phenomena started coming to light.

For instance, can you imagine yourself being in two places at precisely the same moment? Or can you think of an object existing in many forms simultaneously? Can you spin a coin in the clockwise and anti-clockwise directions at the same time? Further, can you imagine two particles of matter, inanimate, but somehow able to communicate through astronomical distances, faster than the speed of light? What if there is no differentiation between the past, present and future? What if you were told that the five-year-old you, and every version

The Mysteries

of you from the past, is not lost but still there?

Magical processes go on in this universe all the time. An entity can be here, there and everywhere at the same time. Energy can transform into particles and matter can change into energy. Particles can disappear on this side of a wall and reappear on the other side. Some inanimate particles can communicate information even when placed in two different galaxies.

Our world is full of things we don't intuitively understand. Time is subjective—it could run slower or faster for you and for me, depending on where we are and whether we are moving. Two twins age differently if one goes to live at high altitudes and the other stays at a lower one. Quite incredibly, in the working of nature, cause and effect might not be chronological but the same—the effect could sometimes come before the cause.

You might think of the above ideas as fictional or metaphysical. Yet, within our bodies, and all around us, such incredible phenomena are happening all the time. In fact, these weird events are the reason why we are able to experience the world the way we do. These 'spooky' actions also caused the one-in-a-zillion chance that we exist on this planet, at this time. We cannot 'see' these things happening, but the universe doesn't wait for our acknowledgement. It never has.

Meanwhile, as human knowledge continues to expand, the number of questions also keep on increasing. What are we—powerful beings or just holographic projections? What exactly is life and why is it limited in time? How did it all begin? Is someone else out there too? Why do we sleep? What are dreams? What is out there in the dark limitless depths of space? Is the world just an illusion? Can we travel to the past? Can we access the future? And, the most nagging of all questions: what is our purpose in life? Most often, these questions are assigned to philosophy, and the latter is frequently used synonymously with the word 'impractical'. So, most of us go about our daily lives ignoring these questions.

We hardly care until death appears on the scene: death of an acquaintance, a neighbour or the most dreaded of all, the death of a loved one. The inconceivable scenario of someone not existing anymore is baffling. The feeling is replicated in profound experiences such as a narrow escape in an accident, a natural calamity, the sight of enormous waves of the ocean or the suffering of terminally ill patients. Many turn to religion for answers, while others explore alternative explanations. One common thing emerges: the awareness of our own existence. Paradoxically, death becomes the driving force for acknowledging life.

From here starts the journey of exploration, the search for the true nature of reality. Along the way, there are observations that the world is full of strange phenomena. Things might not be what they seem to be. There are enigmatic things going on inside every living being as well as inside the rocks and the oceans—and in everything in our visible universe. Take any entity in the observable world: you, a star, a flower or a rock. Beneath the calm surface and clean shapes, zillions of mysterious processes carry on their cosmic dance.

The Mysteries

To add to this dilemma, is the inescapable realization of our own insignificant place in the cosmos. If earth somehow becomes inhospitable to life, it won't be long before we are wiped out, but ants and cockroaches would still be living. We devote our lives to taking pride in our work, families, organizations, cultures and nations. Yet, our entire planet—even our star, the Sun—is just a negligible speck of dust in this universe. There are more stars in the visible universe than there are grains of sand on this earth.[1] Our universe itself is just an insignificant entity on the fabric of the cosmos. It too, will die out. Many such universes have come and gone. Time itself will end. Even with the knowledge of that scale of things, we feel powerful in our individual identities. So, what exactly is the truth of our existence?

It is this ability to question that makes us different from the other forms of life. We can think. We can imagine. We look for meaning in existence. We ask questions. And we are united in that.

The deep questions of existence trouble the mind of the scientist as much as that of the philosopher, the artist or the literary mind. Throughout the long journey of humankind, there have been attempts at understanding the true nature of reality. Among these numerous approaches to search for the truth, two are extraordinary: Vedanta and quantum science.

In the throbbing scientific environment of today, quantum

---

[1] 'How Big Is the Universe ... Compared with a Grain of Sand?', YouTube, https://tinyurl.com/ymx85397. Accessed on 15 September 2023.

science has begun to discover and explain numerous enigmatic concepts. Quite interestingly, there were some minds at least 3,000 years ago as well that had well-rounded explanations of phenomena that are strikingly similar to what quantum science is discovering now. The ancient Vedantic philosophers' detailed explanations are amazingly resonant of what quantum science has discovered regarding the nature of reality. We are probably living in exceptional times, when two widely different approaches to search for the absolute truth are leading to the same goal.

STRANGE CO-TRAVELLERS

Vedantic philosophy and quantum science are like two travellers moving towards the same destination, but in totally different vehicles. The journey is long and the way is unclear, so even as they move with divergent approaches, their paths frequently cross. They even sit down and chat for a while.

Vedantic thought is an ancient, perseverant traveller who has been there, but whose journey will be complete only when every traveller in that direction is escorted to the destination. Quantum science is a young exuberant traveller, excited and grateful even for the tiny wonders that keep unfolding along the path. When the two sit, they often find themselves talking about the same things. Both agree on ideas that would seem fantastically weird to the common person.

It wasn't always a pleasant journey on that path until about a century ago, when quantum science was not around.

The Mysteries

Its older cousin, classical science, was almost always at war with spiritual philosophy, as classical science had defined parameters which philosophy defied. There were countless points of dispute, and to put it simply, the two did not see eye to eye.

All of this changed when the first ideas of quantum mechanics began shaking up the world of science. Quantum explanations were so starkly counter-intuitive, that at first look, they looked more like philosophy or theology rather than science. The most notable feature was an unprecedented open-mindedness to weird possibilities, something that classical science scoffed at.

The meeting of the two travellers is an event of enormous significance for humankind. The ways to reach the ultimate truth can be many, but the goal is the same. The advancement of quantum science makes it increasingly possible for science to find common ground with Vedantic philosophy, and that is unprecedented. That is extraordinary.

Before we begin this fantastic journey, let's give a brief introduction to the two protagonists of this story.

Vedanta

Vedanta comes from the ancient revered texts known as the Vedas, whose origin is dated to more than 3,000 years ago (or even older, by some estimates). The Vedas form the basis of the main Indic spiritual traditions. These profound poetic compositions are compact and concise, and written in ancient Sanskrit. They need some informed decoding to be understood by the modern mind. Various interpretations by learned scholars through the centuries have made the task a little easier.

These texts have a mystic origin. It is believed that at some point in the early stages of humankind—when unmanifested information was floating around in cosmic space—some extraordinary minds in deep states of contemplation could access that celestial information and carefully express it in poetic compositions. These profound aphoristic verses were compiled in the form of the four Vedas: the Rig Veda, Sama Veda, Yajur Veda and Atharva Veda. In the words of Swami Vivekananda, these sages were 'the seers of thought', called *mantra-drashtas* in Sanskrit. The concept sneakily reminds one of the modern thought experiments by many noted physicists, including Einstein, Maxwell and Schrodinger.

It is natural for modern minds to doubt the intellectual capability of people of an ancient era. But contrary to our thinking, the minds in that age were probably sharper than our sharpest ones. According to Dr Sally McBrearty, anthropologist at the University of Connecticut, 'The earliest Homo sapiens probably had the cognitive capability to invent Sputnik, but they didn't yet have the history of invention or a need for those things.'[2]

The authorship of the Vedic verses is not ascribed to

---

[2] Noble Wilford, John, 'When Humans Became Human', *The New York Times*, 26 February 2002, https://tinyurl.com/5ajnwzmd. Accessed on 15 September 2023.

individuals. The main reason is that the knowledge expounded in these texts is considered to be of divine origin, humans are merely the interpreters of that knowledge. However, there are references to some sages who are believed to have contributed to these texts and, notably, there are mentions of a number of female philosophers and commentators who have contributed substantially to Vedic literature.

The Vedas have different layers, with different purposes, though. The 'Karma Kanda' is the part dealing with rituals, sacrifices and the detailed liturgy needed to carry out the same. As the name suggests, these are the 'action' part of the Vedas, which deal with detailed instructions about rituals to be performed to acknowledge the forces of nature. Till date, some of the verses continue as chants during various ceremonies.

The 'Gyana Kanda' of the Vedas includes the Upanishads and this is the part where the true heart of Vedic thought lies. As the word gyan implies, it deals with knowledge. The word Upanishad means coming closer to reality, to that liberating knowledge that destroys false notions. The philosophy of the Upanishads is also known as Vedanta, meaning the highest aim, final message or the end goal of the Vedas. There are 108 Upanishads, out of which 10 are supposed to be the principal ones. The extremely succinct verses in the Upanishads are compelling powerhouses of information. Commentaries upon these are numerous and lengthy, and there have been many consolidated versions, among which the most familiar is the Bhagavad Gita. It presents Vedantic philosophy in a concise and comparatively simplified form.

There is a timeless, universal quality about the Upanishads that makes these relevant to all times. In the words of Swami Paramanada, 'The value of the Upanishads, however, does not rest upon their antiquity, but upon the vital message they contain for all times and all peoples. There is nothing particularly racial or local in them. The ennobling lessons of these scriptures are as practical for the modern world as they were for the Indo-Aryans of the earliest Vedic age.'[3]

Hence, it does not come as a surprise that quite a few Western thinkers, including the pioneers of quantum physics like Erwin Schrodinger and Niels Bohr, found resonance of their ideas in the Upanishads. When the goal is to study the nature of reality, the medium might be different but there are bound to be similar observations.

The philosophy of the Upanishads is essentially spiritual, in contrast with the other layers of the Vedas that are religious in nature. Religion and spirituality are hard to separate from each other because they overlap at too many places, while also remaining essentially different. In a world where everything coexists with everything else, religion and spirituality can also not stay isolated from each other. The two influence each other, hence the two are difficult to explain in isolation from each other.

If spirituality is like water, religion is like ice. Both are made of the same substance, but ice has a definite shape, it has form, and it needs certain conditions in its environment

---

[3]Swami Paramananda (trans.), *The Upanishads*, Prakash Books, 2020, p. 15.

to maintain that state. Water is free flowing—it takes the shape of the container it is in. There are more than 4,000 recognized religions in the world, but only one spiritual quest—the search for the ultimate truth of existence.

There is a striking similarity between the approaches of Vedantic thinkers and quantum scientists. Both are deeply rooted in real experience. Vedanta draws its philosophy from real life observations and analyses each argument on the basis of logic and our empirical experience of the world. The Upanishads are full of open, healthy arguments, where the opposite point of view is addressed respectfully.

Science, by nature, relies on observable data and is invariably rooted in real experience. Needless to say, the progress of science depends upon the scientists' open-mindedness to opposing arguments. In a way, scientists are the greatest believers, because they believe in the laws of nature; they are curious as children to unravel the mysteries of existence; they wonder at the magic that nature spins; and most importantly, the passion in their quest demonstrates their unshakable faith that absolute truth is reachable.

Quantum Science

Quantum science is that recent powerful paradigm shift that has changed the scientific world's understanding of reality forever. As the nineteenth century came to a close, the world of science settled into a solid, deterministic view of the phenomena that happened in the world around us, such as the gravitational force and the laws of motion. The laws could apparently explain the world that we see around us, such as a ball being tossed into the air or the Moon orbiting the Earth.

But when the scientists began probing into the depths of matter, trying to look at its smallest units, they weren't prepared for what they found. The working of nature at the level of subatomic particles was nothing like that of the macroscopic world of large objects. Understanding nature's working at the smallest scale required a whole new approach, a willingness to accept weird possibilities. This realization shook the foundations of the classical understanding of physics.

In the early years of the twentieth century, a series of experiments, theories and observations were slowly moving towards an approach that called for a renewed understanding. This new approach, that studied the nature of reality at the smallest possible scales of subatomic particles, came to be known as quantum mechanics.

In the quantum world, laws are not deterministic but probabilistic. An electron, which is a 100 million times smaller than an atom, can appear as a particle now and as a wave a moment later. The fundamental unit of light, a photon, can be both a wave and a particle at the same time. Everything on the Earth falls towards it due to gravity, but everything else in the universe is speeding away from every other object due to repulsive gravity. Time ticks differently at different places. It took the scientific world quite a while to understand that the quantum world does not function according to the classical understanding of our world.

The Mysteries

On the sidelines of all this excitement, a subtle fact also emerged—this new understanding of the working of our world seemed to increasingly echo what the spiritually-inclined minds of ancient Vedantic philosophers had written thousands of years ago. As just one of the numerous examples, the nature of truth, the basis of all existence, as mentioned in the Mundaka Upanishad: 'It is farther away than the far-off, and It is near at hand in this body.'[4] This is an echo of what quantum mechanics found out about electrons, which can be here, there and everywhere at the same time.

It is incredible how the still-being discovered concepts of the quantum world find resonance in Vedanta—as we will find out in this book. However, the two disciplines have numerous other similarities too. Both are open to discussion, both are self-questioning and both indulge in self-reflection. Both also allow for the possibilities that certain facts cannot be understood by our common cognitive tools—we need to have a certain willing suspension of disbelief, a certain openness to weird possibilities to know the true nature of reality. Both these approaches also seek a unified concept to explain the workings of our world.

As Brian Greene said, 'Quantum mechanics is different. Its weirdness is evident without comparison. It is harder to train your mind to have quantum mechanical tuition,

---

[4]Swami Gambhirananda, *Mundaka Upanishad: With the Commentary of Shankaracharya*, Advaita Ashrama, 1995, p. 147.

because quantum mechanics shatters our personal, individual perception of reality.'[5]

This is why human history should be glad that these two travellers met and bridged many gaps. We are probably living in exceptionally special times, where two seekers of truth can debate like friends, not argue like enemies, and that makes the quest for the ultimate truth even more interesting. Both Vedantic thought and quantum science are extraordinary entities, which challenge the human mind to think beyond the familiar. And to know the nature of ultimate truth, we need to be open to tread unfamiliar paths. 'Those who want to get beyond the ways (of the world), do not walk on roads.'[6]

To access this mesmerizing paradigm, a Vediquant approach is needed—an open-minded exploration of the similarities between Vedanta and quantum science without showing favour or bias towards either of the disciplines. It is a state of mind where preconceived notions are broken to reach a whole new world of absolute truth.

---

[5]'Top 120 Brian Greene Quotes (2023 Update)', *quotefancy*, https://tinyurl.com/bmc57r7e. Accessed on 15 September 2023.
[6]Swami Gambhirananda (trans.), *Eight Upanishads: With the Commentary of Shankaracharya*, Advaita Ashrama, 1989, p. 171.

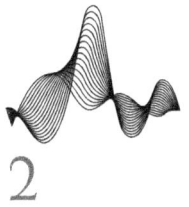

2

Mysteries Deepen

'Which is that thing which having been known, all this becomes known?'[v]

—Mundaka Upanishad

WHAT ARE YOU?

The question seems rhetorical, maybe it's even clichéd for you, but at times, you might have wondered what you *actually* are. Most of us can answer 'Who are you?' as defined by our names, families, faith, nationalities or professions. But to answer 'What are you?', we might say we are humans. So, what is a human? Is it your body, or is it the thoughts in your head? Is it your collection of memories, desires and

---

[7]Swami Gambhirananda (trans.), *Eight Upanishads: With the Commentary of Shankaracharya Vol. II,* Advaita Ashrama, 1992.

secrets? Are you what you think your personality is? If you are religiously inclined, you might say you are mind-body-soul? What is your soul and where is it situated? If you say that you are a combination of all the above factors, what are you when you are not aware of these factors, as in when you are sleeping? When you see yourself in your dream, which one is the real you? What about deep sleep, when you are not even dreaming and are unaware of your body or mind?

Just observe your surroundings for a moment. Where are you? Are you alone? Even if you see other humans, birds or animals around you, you won't be able to *see* everything that exists in your immediate environment. There are microscopic organisms in the air around you, on your table, on your skin and even in your gut. Beyond your address, the entire planet is populated with an estimated 8.7 million species of plants and animals—of which just one species, humans, is 8 billion and counting—and you are just one individual out of those.

However, the planet does not belong to just living creatures. The soil, the air, the rocks, sunlight and alien matter that fell on the Earth—all of those are also inhabitants of this planet. And besides the visible matter, there are waves, radiation and vibrations that are inseparable parts of our existence. Our brain directs every action in our body through electrical impulses. Our body stays alive due to complex chemical processes and super-efficient transportation of energy. Even as you sit unaware, billions of processes inside

Mysteries Deepen

your body are working in perfect tandem to materialize your existence. Your brain is the most complex functioning thing in the universe, yet known, but it is built from just atoms and molecules. Even the inanimate things around you—the chair you are sitting on, the book you are holding—are built up by perfect coordination between atoms and molecules that are communicating and experiencing their individual vibrations at this moment (and at every point in time).

Even if you don't care about the minute details and about the science and the philosophy, the reality of existence affects you. It shapes you, every moment. You are making choices every moment of your life—whether to say something or not; whether to have a full glass of water or just take a sip; whether to feel apathetic or empathetic towards someone… the list is endless. From the smallest things in your life to the most important decisions you take, all of it is continuously contributing to making you what you are. You might have come across people with regrets, people who remark, 'I would never have taken that decision if I knew this would happen.' But how could it be otherwise? That is how life is supposed to be, isn't it?

At this point, the most confusing facts about existence come into the picture: you can see your past, but cannot do anything about it (even if you time travel to the past); you cannot see the future, but you can possibly do anything in it. How can you then decide how to make the right choices? Consider this: a baby who puts its hand into a vessel of hot water doesn't know that hot water can burn skin. If the baby had knowledge of hot water and its dangers, it would have never touched it. But it probably had the knowledge that splashing water is a lot of fun. As the baby grows, its brain is conditioned by various sources of knowledge. As a result, the baby will have a dynamic flow of information telling it what is good or bad. And by the time it becomes an adult, the individual will probably be content with the information in their brain—satisfied that it is a secure deposit to lead life. But is that knowledge enough?

Science unquestionably endeavours to find the correct explanation of phenomena. The Upanishads tirelessly insist that right knowledge, and not the volume of information in the brain, is the key. You must have noticed how you feel inexplicably uneasy when certain thoughts cross your mind, while some other thoughts make you feel strangely calm. You might know a person who stays in a constant state of frustration, and another who smiles more often. Why is it that some people live in a constant state of anxiety and agitation? It's a vicious cycle—inner agitation leads to wrong choices because these choices are driven by a wrong set of knowledge. Wrong choices lead to more stress, and a lifelong trap of dissatisfaction.

But who decides what is the 'right knowledge'? Is there something like 'wrong knowledge' as well? The answer is given by the universe itself, the ever-present entity called existence. Pause for a moment and think. Whatever we think we 'know'—the knowledge that we are proud of—is being falsified by the universe every single moment. Our concept

Mysteries Deepen

of 'correct' could be nature's concept of 'false'. The Sun you see during the sunset is only an optical illusion. The Sun has already dipped below the horizon when you think you can see it. If you immerse a part of a pen or pencil in a glass of water, the part inside the glass looks bent at an angle. In reality, that is not true. If you did not know that the pencil is actually straight, you would have believed that the illusion of the bent pencil was the truth. How many such false ideas exist in our brain?

Optical illusions are of great interest to neuroscientists because they give valuable information about how our brain processes the information that our eyes perceive. There are numerous famous examples, including 'the dress that broke the internet'. An optical illusion makes things appear differently to different people—it could be difference in colour, shape, form or location. Scientifically, we see with our brains, not with our eyes. More importantly, what we see depends on the information stored in our brain. This is why what is apparent is not always true. What we see with our eyes might be entirely different from reality.

Another famous thought experiment is known as Mary's Room. Mary is an exceptional scientist who specializes in vision science and neurophysiology, and knows everything there is to know about the world. Only, she has always lived in a black and white room and she studies the world through a television with a black and white screen. When she comes out of the room and sees other colours, will she learn anything new? For instance, she knows how to describe the colour red scientifically and neurologically, but what will her experience of *seeing* the colour red be?

When you look up at stars in the night sky, you think you are seeing those shiny objects in the present moment, but that's not the truth. Light from even the nearest star system, Alpha Centauri, takes more than four years to reach us. So, you always see a four-year-old version of it. That is because we see an object when light from it reflects back to us, and sends a signal to our brains. Thus, there is nothing around you that you are witnessing in the present. It is in the past already by the time you see it—even if by a few nanoseconds.

Not just this, a postulate in quantum science called the Block Universe Theory tells us that the past, present and future might coexist. So, a two-year-old you and the present you exist at the same time. Both are the real you. In fact, mathematical science allows for the possibility of the arrow of time running backwards. Yet, we experience time moving only towards the future. As we move through life, we get older not younger.

Nature tirelessly throws surprises at all levels. Basic science tells us that if two hydrogen atoms collide, they will bounce off each other. But around 4 billion years ago, in a dense cloud of gas and dust, hydrogen atoms instead of bouncing off started colliding and fusing to create enormous amounts of energy. This led to the birth of our Sun, and that aberration in the behaviour of atoms is the reason there is life on our planet today. It is the reason you and I exist. We think we know stuff, but nature outsmarts us at every step.

Mysteries Deepen

There are Answers

To make sense of it all, the philosophers who understood Vedantic ideas composed the Upanishads primarily as philosophical treatises dealing with the most profound mysteries. They designed the Upanishads as comprehensive manuals to access the right knowledge. Quantum science is on the same path, slowly unfolding the same mysteries that intrigue humankind. Interestingly, the approach is the same: science postulates theories, and then asks nature to validate those theories through the results of the experiments. If the findings of experiments are in agreement with the theory, it is a thumbs up from nature, bringing us one step closer to our understanding of reality. Vedanta presents ideas to you, and then asks you to validate those through your own experience. Realizing the ideas for yourself is considered most crucial in Vedanta.

All creatures function according to their knowledge, according to Vedic thought, and if you have the knowledge of the secrets of the universe, there will be a paradigm shift in how you make choices. The Upanishads are devoted to knowledge of the self, because in Vedantic thought, knowing the self is the same as knowing the truth of the Universe and understanding the ultimate cosmic riddle. Similarly, quantum science strives to explore the working of the world at the minutest of scales in order to discover the mysteries deep inside the basic things, because those basic phenomena lead to all that is present in the universe.

To understand all of this and more, an entirely new, counter-intuitive approach is needed. A journey into the mysterious worlds of Vedanta and quantum science is unlike any other thing that we encounter in our daily lives. Just like a 3D movie can be fully appreciated when one is wearing the required eyewear, Vedanta and quantum science have a prerequisite—the explorer should be ready for counter-intuitive concepts. Else, the entire thing would just be a fuzzy sequence of scenes.

The requirement finds a symbolic, though tenuous semblance in the Bhagavad Gita. When Arjuna expresses a desire to 'see' the ultimate reality, Krishna tells him that it cannot be done through the ordinary vision of a human body. He imparts him *divya drishti* (divine eyesight) to enable him to see the truth of the universe. What Arjuna sees is beyond his wildest imagination—the truth of the entire existence, presented in a flash. Our quest might be longer but the secrets of the cosmos, as asserted by quantum physicists as well, need an approach different from our everyday understanding. Some of the prerequisites to understanding these deep mysteries are as follows.

You Need To Be Open

The Upanishads deal with profound philosophy, but use some of the simplest methods to explain the meaning. One of these methods is storytelling. The Katha Upanishad communicates deep ideas through the story of a little boy Nachiketa, whose determination to learn impresses even

Mysteries Deepen

the God of death, Yama. The latter uses various means to divert the kid's attention. He offers gifts and various pleasures, but Nachiketa is determined to get the answer to his question instead. The deity tests him further, and when he is convinced that the boy is ready to receive the knowledge, he explains to him the deepest of secrets. 'The knowledge of the Self cannot be gained unless the heart of the disciple is open and ready for the Truth... May our questioner be like you, O Nachiketa.'[8]

To get a grasp of the complex ideas of Vedanta and quantum science, you need to suspend disbelief, but maintain a questioning attitude at the same time. You need to be ready to accept surreal-sounding ideas, yet maintain the logical faculties of the mind. Neither pure faith nor pure scepticism can help you in understanding these concepts.

When quantum ideas began to find their place in the twentieth century, scientists realized that they would need to shed their earlier approach and be ready for something entirely unexpected. If they had not been open to newer and stranger possibilities, they wouldn't have been able to explore the quantum world. One of the founders of quantum theory, physicist Niels Bohr—who had remarked that the language of subatomic particles can probably be understood only through the language of poetry—had also commented: 'Those who are not shocked when they first come across

---

[8]Swami Paramananda (trans.), *The Upanishads*, Prakash Books, 2020.

quantum theory cannot possibly have understood it.'[9]

Curiosity Is Vital

Vedanta does not ask for a blind acceptance of what its philosophy is describing, and neither do the scientists. Both acknowledge that curiosity is the shining torch that leads the path through darkness. In one of the loftiest intellectual expressions, the Rig Veda begins with self-questioning: 'Who really knows? Who will here proclaim it? Whence was it produced? Whence is this creation? Gods came afterwards, with the creation of this universe. Who then knows whence it has arisen?'[10]

In the words of Albert Einstein, one of the greatest contributors to modern science: 'The important thing is not to stop questioning. Curiosity has its own reason for existing. One cannot help but be in awe when he contemplates the mysteries of eternity, of life, of the marvellous structure of reality.'[11]

Questioning does not undermine the knowledge that these two great approaches are sharing. It only opens more doors to understanding. This is demonstrated explicitly in

---

[9] Heisenberg, Werner, *Physics and Beyond: Encounters and Conversations*, Harper & Row, 1971.

[10] 'Rig Veda: He Knows, Perhaps He Does Not Know', *Progressive Hindu Dialogue*, 24 June 2020, https://tinyurl.com/yc5m66pu. Accessed on 27 September 2023.

[11] 'Einstein Quotes', *NOVA*, https://tinyurl.com/mwxtjvuv. Accessed on 16 September 2023.

the Bhagavad Gita. The entire discourse is based on questions and answers. Arjuna is not afraid of asking the most probing questions. He expresses doubts, urges Krishna to show proof and scrutinizes every statement of Krishna's that he doesn't understand. In fact, it is the reason why Arjuna is the worthy receiver, the only receiver, of this special knowledge. He is open to learning and he is ready to analyse and question.

Knowing Is Not the Same as Understanding

Knowing a concept academically is different from 'feeling' it. Vedantic philosophers have laid a lot of stress on going beyond words and experiencing the concepts directly. They suggest various methods, including introspection, questioning, dwelling on the concepts and even realization through ordinary activities of daily life. Swami Gambhirananda in his commentary on Mundaka Upanishad points out that true knowledge is 'not merely the assemblage of words found in the Upanishads'.[12] Isa Upanishad reiterates this concept: 'Those who worship or cherish Vidya (knowledge) for mere intellectual pride and satisfaction, fall into greater darkness, because the opportunity which they misuse is greater.'[13]

Just an academic understanding of Vedantic concepts is considered so inadequate that Adi Shankaracharya, one of

---

[12] Swami Gambhirananda (trans.), *Eight Upanishads: With the Commentary of Shankaracharya*, Advaita Ashrama, 1989.
[13] Swami Paramananda (trans.), *The Upanishads*, Prakash Books, 2020, p. 36.

the most influential proponents of Advaita Vedanta, wrote an entire treatise called 'Aparokshanubhuti'. The term means 'direct realization', and the work contains guidelines for an individual to see the truth for themselves.

Vedantic approach mentions three stages necessary for gaining knowledge: *shravana,* which means hearing; *manana*, reflecting upon what was heard; and finally *nidhidhyasana*, which means realizing for oneself. The third step is also translated as meditation or realization. It requires a person to experience for themselves, what they have heard or read. Till then, the understanding is not complete.

This approach finds a striking parallel in the spirit of systematic scientific enquiry, and that is what makes the two seemingly different travellers take notice of each other quite often. The words of Richard Feynman, one of the most well-known physicists, comprehensively sums up the point: 'You can know the name of a bird in all the languages of the world, but when you're finished, you'll know absolutely nothing whatever about the bird... So let's look at the bird and see what it's doing—that's what counts. I learned very early the difference between knowing the name of something and knowing something.'[14]

---

[14]Feynman, Richard P., *'What Do You Care What Other People Think?': Further Adventures of a Curious Character*, Penguin Books Limited, 2007.

Mysteries Deepen

WHY SHOULD YOU CARE?

Human life is like a kitchen full of supplies, with utensils, fuel, grains, vegetables, etc. If you know how to use those resources, you can cook a nourishing meal. Otherwise, your experiments with various resources may or may not yield desirable results. Human existence is blessed with numerous such gifts, which if used properly, can lead to happier, wholesome living.

Have you ever felt that certain choices that you made by copying others had an unsettling effect deep inside you? You might have also noticed that sometimes when you choose a popular course of action, there is something inside of you that tells you it is not correct? Have you felt that shiver of satisfaction when you did something you considered right, no matter what the others were saying? Have you ever felt that ecstatic bliss when you helped someone without expecting anything in return?

How much of our existence do we understand in our routine lives? Probably not even a fraction. Most of us go through our lives looking at only a part of the story, missing the *actual* story. Ignorance makes us believe that what we see is the whole picture. But within the layers of our being, quantum processes are connected with our mind. Both quantum science and Vedanta tell us that our experience is shaped by many subtle factors, not readily visible to our sight. Awareness of those connections can make all the difference. Otherwise, you would have seen life but not felt it.

Both Vedanta and quantum science bring us closer to

our truth, and the beauty is that this knowledge is available to see. You can see, understand and feel it for yourself. You don't have to be a monk or a yogi to do that. The ocean of knowledge is accessible to every individual and it affects different people in different ways, depending upon what you are seeking. One size doesn't fit all, and one approach is insufficient for everyone. That is why Vedanta lays great stress on realizing the knowledge for yourself, and that is also why science strives hard to present evidence before you.

If questions have arisen in your mind, you have already begun the journey. You might not have realized that by being curious you have taken the first steps to elevate your existence.

VIDYA AND *AVIDYA*—THE ETERNAL STRUGGLE

'Those who worship avidya enter into blinding darkness.'[15]

—Isa Upanishad

The greatest struggle in our world has always been between *vidya* and *avidya*, true knowledge and the absence of true knowledge. The Upanishads, through various lines of reasoning, encourage an individual to move from ignorance to knowledge—from avidya to vidya—insisting

---

[15]Swami Gambhirananda (trans.), *Eight Upanishads: With the Commentary of Shankaracharya*, Advaita Ashrama, 1989.

Mysteries Deepen

that ignorance of true knowledge is akin to 'killing the self'. As abstract as this sounds, it can be paraphrased as meaning that ignorance of true knowledge keeps a person away from the truth about existence. Hence, an ignorant person is alive but does not really live. To add to it, any amount of karma will not help. One must go beyond the karma, beyond what is considered religious duties or rites. In his interpretation of Isa Upanishad, Swami Paramananda says: 'Here the Upanishad shows that the only hell is absence of knowledge.'[16]

Avidya primarily means ignorance of true knowledge. It is also a wide term, including various aspects of mundane living like doing something with a desired result in mind. In essence, anything that is less than realizing the absolute truth of the universe is avidya, including limiting yourself to rituals, scriptures and not going beyond those to understand the higher reality. Avidya causes people to believe that the perceivable world around them, including their beliefs and thoughts, is the complete reality. Hence, it prevents a person from reaching out to the deeper, universal truth. It not only stunts the spiritual growth of a person, but also makes the experience of this life unwholesome.

Avidya exists in our world because it is essential. It exists because it is a stepping stone, a necessity. It acts as a stimulant that creates a yearning to come out of darkness. If a person has recognized avidya, they have progressed substantially.

---

[16] Swami Paramananda (trans.), *The Upanishads*, Prakash Books, 2020, p. 31.

However, if a person does not recognize avidya, it gains immense power and veils true reality. As a result, avidya becomes the cause of regression.

It prevents people from rising above what the Upanishads call 'lower knowledge'. The result is destruction of goodness. Avidya encourages hatred by making people believe in their superiority over others; it causes people to believe untruths; it leads to delusions; causes sorrow and grief, among many other subtle things that a common person might not even notice. Its ultimate result is darkness and destruction of the self.

On the contrary, vidya is the key to freedom and a state of perpetual bliss. This is the knowledge about the true nature of reality. It is the realization of the oneness of all existence—a concept that a materialistically-inclined mind (conditioned by karma and avidya) finds hard to grasp. To realize the ultimate truth, ego has to be subjugated and a person under the sway of avidya finds this extremely unpleasant. The advancement from avidya to vidya is found to be difficult, because the Upanishads have a clear requirement, as mentioned in the Isa Upanishad: 'He who sees all beings in the Self itself, and the Self in all beings, feels no hatred by virtue of that realization.'[17]

To remove hatred from the mind, ego has to be subdued. Under the spell of avidya, a person cannot imagine living

---

[17]Swami Gambhirananda (trans.), *Eight Upanishads: With the Commentary of Shankaracharya*, Advaita Ashrama, 1989.

Mysteries Deepen

without their ego. This is because of the false impression that ego gives them their identity.

Mythology, though entirely different in texture from Vedanta, is often efficient at explaining complex concepts through personifications. A mythological character, called Apasmara, is the demon of avidya and perpetually lurks around trying to overshadow knowledge and truth. It can acquire various forms and is generally invisible. Its aim is to induce forgetfulness, so that people forget how to differentiate between good and evil. It casts a spell of avidya. The result is the veiling of the real truth, that activates negative forces (that lead to an illusory belief in falsity, egotism, greed and untruth) and causes the eventual destruction of the self.

But here, the story takes an interesting turn. Since avidya flourishes in this universe, the power of vidya can also be solicited as this is a universe of opposites. One of the ways of doing this is by invoking Shiva, a personal manifestation of Brahman (the Absolute Reality). Shiva is truth and purity, and nothing else in the universe is more powerful. When invoked, Shiva takes the form of Nataraja to control and subdue Apasmara. Interestingly, he chooses not to annihilate it. In Shiva's presence—in effect, in the presence of truth—Apasmara is rendered powerless. The path to truth is laid through experiencing ignorance. The effort is important. Hence, the two coexist. It is up to an individual to break free from ignorance and to elevate oneself.

This powerful verse from Isa Upanishad sums up the whole

Vediquant

thought, like a mystic holding forth a pearl as the answer to everything: 'He who knows these two, vidya and avidya, together, attains immortality through vidya, by crossing over death through avidya.'[18]

---

[18]Ibid. 21.

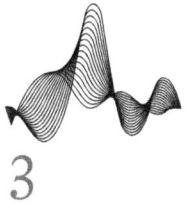

3

One Reality—*Ekam Sad*

'Ekam Sad, Vipra Bahudha Vadanti—Truth is One; }
The wise call it variously.'[19]

The progression from avidya to vidya requires acceptance of the ultimate truth. Any mention of oneness in the modern world is usually perceived as a boring and redundant philosophical chatter that has nothing to do with practicality. It is considered more beneficial to glamorize differences, as that keeps the ecosystem of competition alive and gives a sense of self-worth—hence, feeding the ego. However, if one is on the journey to find the secrets of the universe, ego is strictly prohibited in the baggage. Avidya has its vested interests in keeping people away from the truth, but it is rendered powerless in front of an individual determined to find the truth.

---

[19]Ibid.

A famous hymn from the Rig Veda states that *'Ekam sad; Vipra Bahudha Vadanti* (Truth is one; the wise call it variously).' The Upanishads contain an extremely sophisticated, elaborate and multi-layered explanation of the true nature of reality, and use multifarious expositions to drive home this central idea that there is only one truth that encompasses everything. The complexity of that ultimate truth is expressed in just one word. That word is 'Brahman'. It is pronounced 'brahm' and is not to be confused with the caste tag brahmin or with the god-form Brahma. To understand the concept of Brahman, a number of aspects need to be understood first. To put it in a simplified form, Brahman is the absolute reality which is infinite and without causation. It is self-existent, non-destructible, all-pervasive and without any attributes. It cannot be seen or measured, but everything is a projection of Brahman in Brahman. Nothing is outside of it.

In the quantum science approach to the ultimate truth, the greatest quest is to find that one theory that can explain everything. This includes all the known forces and all the known fundamental particles, along with the phenomena in the observable, macro world. Unlike Vedanta, science does not have a name for it yet, but the term 'unification'—the theory of everything—is loosely used to describe it. Science has arrived at a widely-accepted conclusion that there must be a single reality behind all phenomena.[20]

---

[20]Zhiliang Cao, Henry Gu Cao and Wenan Qiang, 'Theory of Everything', *Frontiers of Astronomy, Astrophysics and Cosmology*, Vol. 1, No. 1, 2015, pp. 33–36.

One Reality—Ekam Sad

The ideas started gaining favour with the dawning of quantum understanding, as it became clearer how reality works at the level of subatomic particles and even inside those micro environments. Initially, the idea perplexed people because the macro world, seen all around us, works differently. To use a classical example, if you throw a ball up in the air, you know it will follow a certain curved path and then fall to the ground due to gravity. But at the same time, every atom in that ball and every atom in the air is witnessing some action. To put it in perspective, 1 cubic centimetre of air has 90 million-million atoms. Each atom of the ball, the air and even you contain subatomic particles or fields—all working in a certain rhythm to materialize the existence of all these entities. The forces of nature, such as the nuclear forces at the micro level and the gravitational forces at the macro level must have something in common—one absolute thing that is guiding them all. It is the search for that super force that makes many scientists hopeful for a single explanation for everything in our universe.

There is a catch, though. Finding the true nature of reality is not like our everyday endeavours. It is extraordinary, requiring an even more extraordinary effort. At the same time, you might intuitively understand it but probably don't feel a need to express it.

As mentioned in the Kena Upanishad, 'It is known to him to whom It is unknown; he does not know to whom It is known. It is unknown to those who know well, and known to those who do not know.'[21]

Like all aphoristic statements of the Upanishads, this profound statement also needs some decoding. It is not meant to be a discouraging remark for seekers. In fact, the entire effort of the Upanishads is directed towards making us understand the true nature of reality. The implied meaning here is that the realization of Brahman is of a nature which cannot be expressed satisfactorily within the limitations of any known language. A similar sentiment is echoed in the famous words of physicist Richard Feynman: 'If you think you understand quantum mechanics, you don't understand quantum mechanics.'[22]

But what is so complicated about understanding the nature of reality? Both these approaches use abstract, complex descriptions that can be hard to grasp at first. If one studies both of them with an unprejudiced curiosity, one can see that the similarity is the result of one basic fact: the true nature of reality (our quest) is probably not perceivable by our ordinary methods. We need to go beyond what is obvious. The two travellers (Vedanta and quantum science) agree on this and the thought is nicely summed up in the words of quantum physicist Brian Greene: '…the Vedas seek something stable, some kind of constant quality underlying the shifting sands

---

[21]Swami Gambhirananda (trans.), *Eight Upanishads: With the Commentary of Shankaracharya*, Advaita Ashrama, 1989.
[22]'Quantum Mechanics', *NewScientist*, https://tinyurl.com/puhbus7r. Accessed on 27 September 2023.

of familiar reality. It is a description that I, and many of my colleagues, would happily use in characterizing the charge of fundamental physics. The disciplines share a common urge to see beyond appearances available to everyday experience.'[23]

CAN A DIVERSE EXISTENCE HAVE THE SAME TRUTH?

You and I are not the same. People of different races look different. People of the same race think and act diversely. You are distinct from the book in your hand. The book is unlike the air around it. The air is different from the grass outside. The rooted grass is not the same as fluid water. Water is distinguishable from earth and the Earth is different from the Sun and the Moon. Our galaxy is not like other galaxies in the solar system. So how can all of these entities have the same truth?

Well, what are you looking at?

And, how are you looking?

Consider this: if you think you recognize yourself, you mean that you can recognize your appearance in the mirror or a photo of yourself, or maybe a verbal description of yourself. What if you were shown only the scans and the X-rays of your body? It would be you, all the same, right?

---

[23]Greene, Brian, *Until the End of Time: Mind, Matter, and Our Search for Meaning in an Evolving Universe*, Penguin Books Limited, 2020, p. 204.

But you are not just that, you would argue. You are your thoughts, your memories and your breath (along with your body). You are right. But how did the brain functions come about in the first place? The air that you breathe—is that exclusive to you? Did you choose the molecules you wanted to be constructed with? It's not that reductionist, you might contend. You also have a consciousness and that differentiates you from everything and everyone else.

Or does it?

How It All Began

To find the first crucial hints towards solving the mystery, we need to take a journey back in time to about 13.8 billion years ago, when our universe was born. Although, that was not the beginning of everything. On the timeline of the cosmos, this time is pretty recent because the cosmos stays busy creating and dissolving universes in a cyclical manner.

The Big Crunch Theory postulates that the beginning of our universe, known as the Big Bang, was probably an event after the wrapping-up of the previous universe—another event in the cycle of events. So, in a way, our universe could be a recycled version of a previous one. When we are dealing with events that far back in time, the human brain has limitations. That the human brain is the most complex and most sophisticated thing yet known, does not help. That leaves us with access to information only as far back as the beginning of our universe. So, our story (in a quantum perspective)

One Reality—Ekam Sad

begins when this universe came into being.

It was the time when there were no living beings, no planets and stars—no matter at all. There was nothing, almost. Somewhere in the infinite nothingness, was a singularity. It was unimaginably small, with zero volume of space and infinite density, and with a peculiar energy that can be described by a scalar-only field. Energy was all there was. At the precise moment, when the conditions were just right (uniformly distributed energy in that region, an extreme rarity), a mysterious force triggered a stupendously rapid expansion of that region of space. Though the nature of this force is unknown, one understanding is that all the forces combined into a single one at that point in time. One plausible candidate force is repulsive gravity. Yes, gravity doesn't just attract. It can push things apart too, in the rarest of conditions. That condition was enough to spark what is known as the Big Bang. In an incredible billionth-of-a-billionth-of-a-billionth of a second after the spark, the miniscule speck expanded to become a universe. We don't know how big our universe is, but we can 'see' things in it as far as 540 sextillion miles (which is 54 followed by 22 zeroes). And that is obviously just a small part of a still-expanding universe.

This often-heard description seems so dramatic that you might dismiss it as a wild guess, but the cosmos sneakily left evidence of the event, which we can see 13.8 billion years later as well. This evidence is in the form of whispers that float about in space, and can be detected by devices on Earth. Its scientific name is 'Cosmic Microwave Background

Radiation', and one does not always need powerful equipment to detect it. If you were born at a time when you could see an old-style analog TV, you might remember the 'snow' or the cloud of random dots that appeared on the screen when there was no transmission signal. Part of that snow could have been your TV catching the cosmic remains of the Big Bang.

If that sounds uncanny, here is another fact. Every atom in your body and every atom in everything around you has come from that one breathtaking cosmic event. In a series of phenomena that lasted billions of years, the energy in that primitive region of space formed matter, and matter constitutes all that is visible to us today.

The first major events after that expansion happened in a fraction-of-a-fraction of a second. The expansion formed an extremely chaotic and super-hot plasma—conditions in which no particles could exist. There was no matter, no antimatter, only an 'inflaton field' occupying that expanding space. Another mysterious force or condition then caused the inflaton field to give rise to a spray of primordial particles (nothing like the current subatomic particles). These particles went through successive stages to form protons, neutrons and electrons—the primary constituents of all atoms in the universe.

To offer clarity to the uninitiated, all matter in the universe—whether solid, liquid or gas—is made of atoms. These atoms are so small that they cannot be seen even with the most powerful microscopes. One square centimetre of your skin has 6 million cells, and each cell has more than a trillion atoms. Yet, atoms are not the smallest part of matter. They are made of subatomic particles, which in turn are made of quarks. Quantum science has taken us inside of the quarks as well.

Immediately after the rapid expansion, the ferocious energy in that region of space—the temperature being more than 1 billion kelvins—prevented the subatomic particles from coming together to form atoms. Anything that was formed was quickly destroyed.

But then something magical happened. As the temperature dropped, the primordial force started appearing in different manifestations. The strong nuclear force made it possible for protons and neutrons to come together to form the nuclei of atoms. Without this force, no matter would have ever been formed, because protons are positively charged and they wouldn't really sit together. Then as the environment cooled further (though the temperature was still several thousand kelvins), another manifestation of the primary force appeared in the form of the electromagnetic force. This force caused negatively charged electrons to hover around positively charged nuclei. The two were held together by this force, and the first type of atoms were formed. These were the hydrogen atoms, the simplest atoms in our universe.

Scattered through the plasma, clouds of hydrogen gas began to cluster and, in certain cases, these clouds started getting denser. This was made possible by a third manifestation of the original force—the gravitational force. The extreme conditions led to a crushing together of hydrogen atoms to form helium atoms. In the process, a tremendous amount of energy was released. Wherever this happened, stars were born.

With the further cooling of the cosmic chaos, nuclear processes increased and that resulted in the formation of more types of atoms. Very large stars continued the fusion process further to form successively heavier elements—carbon, oxygen and lastly, iron. The other heavy elements were formed in the ultra-dense conditions of collapsing stars or during collisions of neutron stars. In time, the atoms came together to form molecular clouds. In other words, every type of atom that we are made of was created in the stars.

Around 10 billion years of this spectacular cosmic show went by, and there was no sign of our solar system, till our Sun was formed. Compared to the other stars, our Sun is small (the first stars were a thousand times larger than the Sun) and young—just around 4.5 billion years old. A giant rotating disc of stellar dust of elements and gases formed our galaxy, within which our solar system formed. The gases and elements coalesced into planets around the Sun and the latter's pull is sufficiently strong to keep eight planets and some exoplanets revolving around it. Among these planets, the Earth happened to be just at the right distance from the fiery Sun—the perfect place to have our kind of life. A little tweak in the process, and we would not have existed.

It was not always smooth for Earth, when it formed. It either started its life like a hot ball of flowing lava and toxic gases filling its atmosphere, or as an extremely wet and inhospitable sphere. It was constantly hit with meteors and even had a collision with a planet called Theia. The latter was destroyed but the material that blew out from this collision formed the Moon. The collision turned out hugely in favour of the Earth because it tilted the Earth's axis by about 23 degrees, and set the perfect stage for seasons to happen. If the Earth had no seasons, life would have been a struggle for food and a perpetual grim battle with diseases. A collision made our home more comfortable.

As Earth's conditions further stabilized, soon came the first forms of life and in time, more complex organisms evolved. There are billions of species of organisms on Earth. Yet, if you could peer inside any cell of any organism, you would see the same activities going on. The molecules, atoms and ions working in perfect tandem to harvest, store and transport energy. You would see impeccably laid out DNA strands holding encoded information about that organism. Though you wouldn't want to believe that you have anything in common with the people you dislike, you can't really change this ubiquitous reality—every living thing on this planet came from the same ancestor, and at a deep level their bodies continue to work in the same quantum way. Even grander is the fact that everything, visible or invisible, in this universe came from that one entity that was there in the beginning.

Science has thus unravelled how a mysterious, primitive energy was present at the time of the beginning of this universe. It was just a field, a force or just energy. Space did not even exist at that time, and probably time (as we know it) did not exist. Science works on empirical evidence, and there are meticulously worked out explanations in quantum physics—accurate to a whopping 10 decimal places. There are explanations about the ways in which that energy triggered, in its own field, the beginning of this universe and manifested itself as different forces, transforming energy into matter (atoms and molecules). There are precise mathematical calculations about the timeline of this universe, from the formation of the first atoms to the formation of known stars and planets and the evolution of life on Earth. To put it simply, energy manifested into matter and some of that matter developed brains and became sentient.

But that is obviously not the whole story. This is just one part of it.

LOOKING THROUGH ANOTHER LENS

Truth has a way of appearing in myriad forms. Through the centuries, differently conditioned minds have been trying to interpret truth in their own way. Language, the best medium of communication, also has great limitations—especially when one is dealing with two periods of time separated by thousands of years. Thus, it would be incorrect to draw word-to-word parallels between quantum science and Vedantic thought. However, the import or the implied meaning is jaw-droppingly similar.

The Nasadiya Sukta of Rig Veda, also known as the Hymn of Creation, has a poetic interpretation of that profound moment in time:

One Reality—Ekam Sad

> There was neither non-existence nor existence then;
> Neither the realm of space, nor the sky which is beyond [...]
>
> There was neither death nor immortality then;
> No distinguishing sign of night nor of day [...]
>
> Darkness there was at first, by darkness hidden;
> Without distinctive marks...[24]

It is impossible to ignore the outstanding similarity between scientific explanations and the ideas expressed in this hymn. Neither 'existence nor non-existence' echoes the 'zero energy' of the universe mentioned by Stephen Hawking. 'Neither death nor immortality' echoes the events in the early cosmos where particles continuously kept on appearing and getting annihilated. Before the first subatomic particles could form, this rapid creation and annihilation was happening cyclically. There were no stars—hence, no sources of light—so there was 'no distinguishing sign of night nor of day'. There were no distinctive features of that state of the universe, not even space, leave alone matter and particles. But then, some entities started manifesting. As further mentioned in the Nasadiya Sukta of the Rig Veda, 'That which, becoming, by the void was covered; That One by force of heat came into being...'[25]

---

[24]'The Creation Hymn of Rig Veda', *Vinaire's Blog*, 8 April 2011, https://tinyurl.com/4hyc8ff7. Accessed on 27 September 2023.
[25]Ibid.

Mundaka Upanishad mentions a similar idea: 'Through knowledge (tapas) Brahman increases in size. From that is born food (the unmanifested). From food evolves Prana (Hiranyagarbha); (thence the cosmic) mind; (thence) the five elements; (thence) the worlds; (thence) the immortality that is karmas.'[26]

Tapas is interpreted variously as heat, energy, information or knowledge using which Brahman increases in size, just as the primordial universe inflates using its inherent bits of information to make the formation of manifested forms possible. The term 'food' in the Upanishads has a spiritual connotation. It is the means through which the manifest come into being from the unmanifest. For science, these are mysterious 'messengers' or 'force-carriers' that caused the forces to act in a certain way so that the elements could be formed, leading to the formation of galaxies and living creatures as we see them now. Thus, the Vedantic ideas of the beginning of this universe are undeniably similar to what science has discovered.

According to Vedanta, there is one ever-present reality—Brahman—that is not born, but gives rise to various manifested forms within itself. It is just like an expanding universe that gives rise to matter, structure and living beings—all inside of it and of its own accord. Consequently, whatever is contained in the universe is, in essence, Brahman itself (expressing itself in myriad forms).

---

[26]Swami Gambhirananda (trans.), *Eight Upanishads: With the Commentary of Shankaracharya Vol. II*, Advaita Ashrama, 1992, p. 85.

One Reality—Ekam Sad

Here comes another twist. Brahman is not limited to everything that we can 'see'. From near nothingness at the beginning of the universe to the current time, we live in a universe that is expanding at an ever-increasing pace and is still full of things. We see much of it on our planet and beyond it, as shimmering objects in the night sky. Interestingly, all that we can observe in our universe—from the stuff we see around us, to the most distant galaxies recorded through powerful equipment—constitutes only 5 per cent of the universe. This 5 per cent is contained in something that is invisible to us, but is definitely there. It has been calculated that 27 per cent of that mysterious space is something called 'dark matter'. What about the remaining 68 per cent? It is supposed to be something called 'dark energy', and currently we don't really understand it. We do know that dark energy is probably the reason why the galaxies are moving away from each other. It 'stretches' the fabric of space-time to make that happen. So, everywhere we look in the universe, everything visible or invisible is a form of that primordial entity with which it all began. Even before the 'beginning', that entity was present. Only, we cannot see that far back in time.

As the Mundaka Upanishad mentions: 'All this that is in front is but Brahman, the immortal. Brahman is at the back, as also on the right and the left. It is extended above and below, too. This world is nothing but Brahman, the highest.'[27]

---

[27] Swami Gambhirananda, *Mundaka Upanishad: With the Commentary of Shankaracharya*, Advaita Ashrama, 1995, p. 135.

Now comes a natural question. Is Brahman the same as the concept of God? The Upanishads refer to the true nature of reality as 'Brahman', 'the Self' or simply as 'That'. Along with this, the sound 'Om' is supposed to represent Brahman, because it encompasses the entire range of sound articulation by all creatures, from the sound of 'A' to 'U' to 'M', 'A' and 'U' together in Sanskrit form the sound 'O'. The words 'God', 'Ishvara', 'Hiranyagarbha', 'Purusha' or the names of deities, refer to the absolute reality qualified by attributes and specifications. Though some commentators use the words Brahman and God interchangeably, the concept of 'God' or any synonym of it, gives a name, shape and attributes to the entity and hence converts it into a personal God. This is a useful tool in many ways because it makes the concept relatable, but the Upanishads insist that Brahman cannot be defined in known parameters. To resolve this issue, two forms of Brahman are generally accepted: *sagun* Brahman, the one with attributes such as a name and form; and *nirgun* Brahman, the one without attributes. The former is also true (a part of the truth), but the higher reality is considered to be Brahman that cannot be described in terms of attributes.

Whatever name we assign, the universe we live in has one reality that works like magic. Strange things happen. Energy becomes matter, matter emits energy, the unmanifested gives rise to manifested reality, similar particles throughout the universe obey the same principles, one kind of particles change into another and surprises spring up (like hydrogen atoms inside the Sun started combining instead of bouncing off each other). That brings us to the next step in solving the mystery. What are the secrets that Brahman, the one unified grand force, hides inside it?

Is everything as it appears to be?

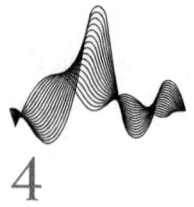

4

Is Everything as It Appears to Be?

'What indeed is here is there; what is there, is here likewise...'[28]

'The Self is subtler than the subtle, greater than the great...'[29]

—Katha Upanishad

The absolute reality, Brahman, the Self or the all-pervading consciousness—whichever name we choose to describe the nature of reality—is subtle, so much so that all the tools of expression (including language) are insufficient to describe it. At the minutest level, it is the same everywhere, whether it is the fundamental reality of humans, a blade of grass or even empty space. Its nature

---

[28] Swami Gambhirananda (trans.), *Eight Upanishads: With the Commentary of Shankaracharya*, Advaita Ashrama, 1989.
[29] Swami Paramananda (trans.), *The Upanishads*, Prakash Books, 2020, p. 87.

Is Everything as It Appears to Be?

is indistinguishable in every bit of matter in the universe. Hence, your fundamental reality is the same as the dust on the side of the road, and also the brightest stars in the sky—hence the words 'what is there, is here likewise'. The reason that everything appears different is because this one entity manifests into different forms. In essence, everything is that one Brahman—there is nothing that is not it.

Due to its subtle nature, it cannot be perceived by the senses, in the way we see the objects around us or even under powerful microscopes. However, it is discernible by the effect it has on the observable world. The basic nature of reality is thus, almost invisible to humans, making it 'subtler than the subtle'. At the same time, it is 'greater than the great' because it is the infinite reality with limitless potential that makes the world possible. Nothing can be more powerful because without it existence is not possible.

As we move from exploring the fundamental nature of reality in the spiritual perspective to exploring it in the quantum physics perspective, there is almost an overlap of metaphysical ideas. The boundaries get blurry and, quite surprisingly, science seems to be talking the language of mysticism. Conventional ideas break down here, and descriptions start flowing like poetry.

As Niels Bohr said, 'Everything we call real is made of things that cannot be regarded as real.'[30] Or as Erwin

---

[30] 'Niels Bohr Quotes', *goodreads*, https://tinyurl.com/4azjckft. Accessed on 16 September 2023.

Schrodinger remarked: 'What we observe as material bodies and forces are nothing but shapes and variations in the structure of space.'[31] As surprising as these statements would appear to be, coming from two of the greatest physicists of all times, what they are referring to is the most revolutionary discovery of modern times—the unity of our quantum reality.

Humans are conditioned to believe that everything is made of particles, however small. We would like to imagine that if we take any object and cut it down to the smallest possible unit, till we cannot tear it further, we would expect to find some kind of basic building blocks. That is right, in a way. All matter is made up of atoms. An atom in turn contains electrons that are orbiting around a nucleus containing protons and neutrons. As mentioned previously, these are made of still smaller particles called quarks. In all, the standard model has no less than 17 subatomic particles that interact in various ways to form matter as we see it.

Here comes the surprise. What if you were told that these particles are not particles at all, but just fields or vibrations? In other words, if you could see and touch subatomic particles, none of these would appear to you as solid, well-defined micro things. You can't hold a subatomic particle, but if you could you would see that it has no definite shape or form. At the same time, this abstraction could also present itself as a well-defined particle in certain conditions. This revolutionary

---

[31]'Erwin Schrodinger Quotes', *BrainyQuote*, https://tinyurl.com/4bmbemkf. Accessed on 16 September 2023.

Is Everything as It Appears to Be?

discovery in the early part of the twentieth century totally transformed our understanding of the physical world and brought it closer to Vedantic thought.

NON-DUAL DUALITY—THE WAVE-PARTICLES

Here is the idea that transformed science forever: every particle exhibits wave-like properties. It is not limited in time. It is not as if a particle turned into a wave cannot come back. A wave can exhibit particle-like properties and vice-versa, for eternity, really. What is more shocking is that the chances of an entity being a particle and a wave exist at the same time, in every moment, till the entity decisively appears as one of those. In other words, we can say that it exists as a particle and a wave at the same time.

This, of course, is in total contrast to what we see around us. If we were to imagine a particle as a glass marble with a definite spherical shape, the wave could be thought of as a waft of air—felt as an abstract something but not seen. A wave, by definition, is a vibration or a disturbance in a medium that carries energy from one point to the other without the movement of particles of matter. So, if we imagine our reality at the tiniest possible level, it would be a surreal picture of energy appearing and disappearing and sometimes materializing as noticeable entities. It is a cosmic drama playing inside of us, in every moment in time and at every point in space.

The beauty of the scientific mind is that it does not stop probing when it is in awe of something. Wave-particle duality has been studied meticulously, and proven time and again by scientists all over the world.[32] The first subatomic particles discovered to be having wave-particle duality were the electrons. The famous double-slit experiment, that has been done numerous times since the first one, is a stunning demonstration of this enigmatic concept.

HERE, THERE AND EVERYWHERE

The double-slit experiment has been done using photons, electrons and even atoms. Every time, the results were the same. This is how it is done. Imagine that you create a set up for a game in which you have to throw tennis balls at a wall some distance from you. You have to put up a barrier of some kind (a thick curtain or a cardboard screen) to mask the wall and provide only two slits in it. When you throw a ball, it will pass through one of the slits and hit the wall behind. But can you imagine a single ball going through both the slits at the same time? Bizarre? This is what happens in the double-slit experiment.

Electrons are shot through a barrier containing two slits, so that they pass through the slits and leave a mark on the screen located behind the barrier. Conventionally, we would expect each electron to pass through either of the slits and

---

[32] Padavic-Callaghan, Karmela, 'Wave–Particle Duality Quantified for the First Time', *physicsworld*, 1 September 2021, https://tinyurl.com/k37pmfdb. Accessed on 27 September 2023.

Is Everything as It Appears to Be?

leave a mark on the screen just behind the slit through which it came. Instead, what is observed is that each electron passes through both the slits at the same time, and as a result instead of getting two linear bands on the screen, we get a pattern of light and dark bands. This is undoubtedly indicative of the electron having behaved as a wave, and not as a particle.

At a time when electrons were thought of as solid particles, these results were unbelievable. If the ball in your game was the size of an electron, it would transform into waves before hitting the barrier and the waves would pass through both the slits. Quantum physics proposed a solution to this strange observation: electrons should be defined by probability waves. An electron exists in all the probable positions at the same time—with the crests of the waves denoting high probability of finding an electron there, and a trough in the wave denoting the least probability of finding an electron in that position. The famous Schrodinger equation can predict with certainty the probabilities of the electron being found in different positions. In quantum physics, equations are like aphorisms of the scriptures—they carry within them encoded messages to address problems.

Wave-particle duality is exhibited by all subatomic particles. It is as if a similar programme directs all particles though they appear to be different. Thus, at the quantum level, reality operates like Brahman. As mentioned in the Katha Upanishad: '…as bodiless in the midst of bodies, as permanent in the midst of the impermanent, and as great and pervasive...'[33] In the words of Werner Heisenberg, 'The atoms or elementary particles themselves are not real; they form a world of potentialities or possibilities rather than one of things or facts.'[34]

Reality at the quantum level, in the form of subatomic particles, is thus bodiless (without form or shape). It is pervasive, universal and true for every wave particle. It is called great because on its actions depends the existence of everything. It is permanent, like an electron that is always a part of an atom but also exists in its own impermanence—as a wave now and a particle then. It is like the permanent Brahman existing in impermanent beings as Atman (pronounced 'aatma'). Reality is all-pervasive, though the particle nature might be temporary. Wave-particle duality is true for all particles, hence making this universe a place of infinite potentialities. The empirically observed physical world is defined by things or facts, whereas its true nature is only a set of possibilities. This echoes Heisenberg's words that atoms and particles themselves are not real. The true nature of reality is of potentiality.

That infinite potential is Brahman, present in all material and subtle things in the universe. Its basic nature is unsullied by the countless manifestations it acquires. In beings, it is

---

[33] Swami Gambhirananda (trans.), *Eight Upanishads: With the Commentary of Shankaracharya*, Advaita Ashrama, 1989, p. 156.
[34] 'Notable Quotes on Quantum Physics', *QuantumEnigma*, https://tinyurl.com/2p9wjbpz. Accessed on 16 September 2023.

Is Everything as It Appears to Be?

referred to as the witness consciousness, the pure consciousness or the essence of existence. One name that is commonly used is Atman—the capitalization is a recognition of Atman being a reflection of Brahman. In non-living things, it is the same existence that is manifest in the form of fields, forces, space, dark matter and dark energy.

MYSTERIOUS SUPERPOSITION

Closely related to wave-particle duality is one of the most astonishing features of quantum physics—superposition. Two quantum particles are said to be in superposition when they exist in two opposite states at the same time. Thus, a subatomic particle could be spinning in clockwise and anti-clockwise directions at the same time. An atom can exist in a state of excitation and non-excitation at the same time. And not just particles and atoms, any physical system can be described by many possible states. There can be an infinite number of states that a system can be found in, and the original state is considered a superposition of all possible states.

This idea was famously demonstrated through a thought experiment by Erwin Schrodinger, known as Schrodinger's cat. A hypothetical cat is put in a sealed box along with a radioactive material that has a 50 per cent chance of releasing a lethal substance in the time frame of an hour. After an hour, when the box is opened, the cat could either be dead or alive. This is where quantum mechanics comes into the picture. Till the box is opened, the cat is simultaneously dead and alive. It is in a superposition of two states.

Before this idea can sink in, quantum mechanics throws another one at us. A particle can be in two different positions at the same time. It is like saying you could be in your living room right now, and also at your workplace. None of those is a false you. Both the people are you. The idea is so counter-intuitive, that one would dismiss it offhand. However, this entire universe is made up of quantum particles, and the latter have this bizarre tendency of being in more than one place at a time and also exist in two different states at the same time.

Superposition happens all around and within us, all the time. Take for example, photosynthesis—that phenomenal process responsible for transforming the Sun's energy into the energy that sustains living organisms on Earth. The Sun's energy reaches Earth in the form of photons which are like packets of light energy. Tiny organelles present in green plants tap these photons and convert it into chemical energy in the form of food, also releasing oxygen in the process. If photosynthesizing plants were not there, other living beings (like us) wouldn't exist.

The process of photosynthesis is incredibly precise and requires tapping and transporting photons to a spot called the 'energy centre' in the chloroplast. The photons move at a speed that is difficult to visualize through classical understanding. They must be transported really quickly before they dissipate. This presumably happens through quantum superposition. Photons are transferred through every possible route in the

Is Everything as It Appears to Be?

plant, simultaneously. That explains the unbelievable efficiency of the process.

Even within our bodies, quantum processes are happening every micro second. Every cell of the body is witness to processes that are still being studied for better explanations. A quantum explanation now seems feasible in the cases which appeared to be mysterious earlier. Quantum biology is a very young field of study, but as it continues to mature it promises to unlock the mysteries of a number of mechanisms that classical science is not able to.

One exciting prospect is studying quantum superposition through the human eye. The human eye has the ability to detect a single photon, and meticulous experiments are going on to find out if the human eye can detect a photon in a superposition state. In addition, exchange of ions and energy in human cells takes place at incredibly low time scales (something like billionths of a second). That makes quantum superposition a good candidate to be included in the study.

Now, if all things are basically made up of quantum parts, why can't we see superposition happening around us? Why can't you be here and on the Moon at the same time? Why is the book in your hand solid, and not appearing to you as waves? The scientific explanation is that even though at the micro level entities display quantum features, at the macro level those features are not visible. Even at the microscopic scale, the scientific answer is bizarre. Well, this is quantum mechanics. It says that an entity exists in all states of superposition at the same time, but as soon as it is observed there is a collapse of the states. An electron would go on roaming around as a wave, but as soon as you or I observe it, it collapses to appear as a particle. Does that also remind you of sudden mood shifts in babies?

There is a technical term for this in quantum physics: decoherence. Since basically all quantum particles are waves, they appear in a state of superposition when there is coherence between their parts. Large objects like a chair do not appear to be in this state because the coherence between its wave functions has broken down, making the object appear in a single state. Till an entity is seen or observed, it remains in superposition of various states but as soon as we observe it, it collapses into an object. To put it in simplified terms, everything exists as a wave till we see it or try to measure it. Think of it. It might make you want to see the world in an entirely new perspective.

SPECTACULAR SUPERPOSITION IN VEDANTA

Amazingly, Vedantic thought has been extremely comfortable with the idea of superposition. In fact, superposition is highlighted to explain the non-dual nature of apparent duality. While in quantum science, we talk in terms of particles, waves, fields and states, in Vedanta we talk of the basic nature of reality denoted by the single word Brahman.

The following verse from Isa Upanishad might inspire

Is Everything as It Appears to Be?

awe in many: 'That moves, That does not move; That is far off, That is very near; That is inside of all this, and That is also outside all this.'[35]

An atom can be in a state of excitation (high energy state) or non-excitation at the same time, like Brahman appearing as various possibilities in all of existence. Though the Self in itself is motionless, yet it seems to move. It is as if the observer's presence or the interference of the environment causes a collapse of the superposition, making the entity appear to move (while in reality it coexists in both the states). In another interpretation, if there is one entity—Brahman pervading all of existence—and if everything is contained in that single entity, it need not move. At the same time, it would appear to move in various objects. This also bears an uncanny resemblance to Hugh Everett's theory of the Universal Wave Function. The theory describes a quantum state of the entire universe. It is treated as the fundamental entity of existence.

'That is far off, That is very near.' The superposition of the two states of being close by and also very distant, is a state of the Self. It exists in both the states at all times. Yet, when we look at anything in the world, we can see it only locally. In the absence of true knowledge, the human mind is not conditioned to recognize the simultaneously existing states of that entity. Yet, as Vedantic commentators say—with

---

[35]Swami Gambhirananda (trans.), *Eight Upanishads: With the Commentary of Shankaracharya*, Advaita Ashrama, 1989.

knowledge, one can gradually understand that the Self is here and it is there too.

The third state described above, 'inside of all this, and also outside all this', is self-explanatory. The same entity exists in the minutest parts of your being as well as in the 'outer' world that you see and feel with your senses. Apparent duality is present everywhere, but it is only two simultaneously existing states of one entity.

As mentioned in the Taittiriya Upanishad, 'In the beginning all this was but the unmanifested (Brahman). From that emerged the manifested. That Brahman created Itself by Itself. Therefore, It is called the self-creator.'[36] It also mentions, 'That (Brahman), having created (that) entered into that very thing. And having entered there, It became the formed and the formless, the defined and the undefined, the sustaining and the non-sustaining, the sentient and the insentient, the true and the untrue. Truth became all this that there is. They call that (Brahman) Truth.'[37]

The Upanishads thus present a striking picture of superposition, of two apparently opposing states existing at the same time. While superposition itself is difficult to grasp, there are even spookier, weirder things in quantum science. What is astonishing is that even those spooky actions find resonance in the Upanishads.

---

[36]Swami Gambhirananda (trans.), *Eight Upanishads: With the Commentary of Shankaracharya Vol. II*, Advaita Ashrama, 1992.
[37]Ibid. 344.

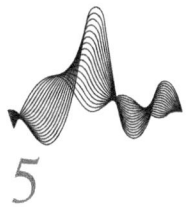

5

Spooky Actions

> *'That is inside all this, and
> That is also outside all this.'*[38]
>
> —Isa Upanishad

Teleportation. Telepathy. Being in more than one place at a time. These ideas are the stuff of science fiction and in many cases mystical tales too. In popular culture, these concepts exist in a romanticized, hyped form that give them an air of fantasy. However, such phenomena do happen, here and now (all around us) and are perfectly explainable with the help of quantum science. At the same time, Vedanta also has clear, comprehensive exposition of such concepts. At first look, these ideas sound so weird that many

---

[38]Swami Gambhirananda (trans.), *Eight Upanishads: With the Commentary of Shankaracharya*, Advaita Ashrama, 1989.

quantum physicists had difficulty accepting them. However, students of Vedanta are familiar with ideas of this nature and accept these with comparative ease.

QUANTUM ENTANGLEMENT

The first of these is what Einstein famously called 'spooky action at a distance'. The scientific name is quantum entanglement. It basically means that if two entities interact (interactions are happening at the quantum level everywhere), and are then separated even by the largest of distances they are somehow able to communicate with each other in a way that the state of one will always be entangled with the state of the other. If the state of one entity changes, the state of the other will change automatically. And this means—and it is an incredible proposition—that information between the two entities is exchanged faster than the speed of light. And nothing is known to travel faster than light. The entities somehow instantaneously share information and remain in an entangled state.

To take an often-quoted example, imagine that two electrons are taken from an entangled state and somehow put into separate boxes. Of the entangled pair, one of the entangled electrons has a 'spin up' (clockwise) and the other has a 'spin down' (anti-clockwise), and no one knows the contents of the boxes. You send one of the boxes to a friend in Mumbai and the other to a friend in New York. When the friend in Mumbai opens and measures the spin of the electron, she finds it to be a spin up. The friend in New York will invariably find the electron with a spin down. The two electrons will have opposite spins even if the situation is reversed, or even if the boxes are sent to the opposite regions of the universe.

In quantum entanglement, a mysterious, faster-than-light communication takes place between two entangled particles. The process itself is not clear, as of now, but science is making progress towards a better understanding. Decoherence is one of the possible explanations for entanglement. Physicists are trying to find out if larger objects can also demonstrate quantum entanglement.[39] Earlier experiments with photons have been successful, and scientists are making efforts to gradually increase the size of the particles and observe entanglement. One such experiment was done with small diamond crystals placed 15 cm apart. Scientists could successfully entangle the quantum states of the two diamonds. In another experiment, physicists could observe entanglement between two unlike objects—a cloud of atoms and a dielectric membrane. Quite incredibly, entanglement and superposition have been exploited to build quantum computers.

In 2019, scientists were able to click a picture of an entangled pair of photons—the first ever picture of its kind. Of

---

[39]Matson, John, 'Quantum Entanglement Links 2 Diamonds', *ScientificAmerican*, 1 December 2011, https://tinyurl.com/kcx9rucd. Accessed on 27 September 2023; Ratner, Paul, 'In Quantum Entanglement First, Scientists Link Distant Large Objects', *BigThink*, 30 September 2023, https://tinyurl.com/3tctwnn9. Accessed on 27 September 2023.

course, it required special conditions and special equipment, but the result was stunning.

The concept is hard to grasp, but quantum entanglement is real. The 2022 Nobel Prize in physics is a landmark in the understanding of (what the Nobel Prize website calls) 'ineffable effects of quantum mechanics'. The prize has been awarded to three physicists who have been working on quantum entanglement. They are Alain Aspect, Anton Zeilinger and John F. Clauser. The official press release of this award is remarkably entitled 'Entangled States—From Theory to Technology'.[40] Zeilinger's group has also demonstrated quantum teleportation, in which the quantum state of one particle can be moved to another particle at a distance.

QUANTUM TUNNELLING

Along with these spooky qualities of the nature of reality, there is something even spookier called quantum tunnelling. Imagine that you are standing in a park, facing a solid wall (10 ft high and as much wide) that has no doors and openings. If you want to go to the other side of the wall, you would either have to navigate your way through the left or right of the wall, or climb up a ladder on this side and then use another ladder to come down on the other side. That would require time and energy. If the wall was part of a

---

[40]'Entangled States – From Theory to Technology' *The Nobel Prize*, https://tinyurl.com/4ewyzzd5. Accessed on 27 September 2023.

room, you would not have been able to navigate around it. However, if you knew how to quantum tunnel, you could be on the other side of the wall by magically passing through it (without causing even a crack in it and without hurting yourself even a bit).

Or imagine riding a bicycle right through the wall to the other side, without hurting yourself, damaging your bike or causing even a chink in the wall. This sounds bizarre, but it happens in the Sun, and it happens all the time in the cells in our body.[41] Particles are somehow able to 'tunnel' though an otherwise impenetrable barrier. What tunnelling basically means is that things are able to penetrate or cross impossible hurdles or energy barriers, which otherwise are not passable. So, tunnelling causes a piece of matter to beckon its wave-like properties to cross over the barrier.

As outlandish as this idea is, it raises more questions that shake the very foundation of our basic scientific understanding of reality. It suggests that faster-than-light travel is possible. It also raises questions about our understanding of the concept of time. Quantum tunnelling, thus, is another surprise that nature puts in front of us.

However, it is not so surprising for those who understand the Upanishadic concepts of reality, time and space. Consider this verse from the Isa Upanishad: 'It is unmoving, one, and faster than the mind. The senses could not overtake It, since

---

[41]Devault, Don, 'Quantum Mechanical Tunnelling in Biological Systems', *Quarterly Reviews of Biophysics*, Vol. 13, No. 4, November 1980, pp. 387–564.

It had run ahead. Remaining stationary, It outruns all other runners, It being there…allots or supports all activities.'[42]

The Upanishads are comfortable with the idea of entanglement and tunnelling (though it does not mention these concepts), primarily because they consider the seat of all reality to be in Brahman. This is expressed through scores of definitions—among which the most striking ones are the ones dealing with paradoxes. The basic idea is this: since everything is Brahman and everything exists in Brahman, all the apparent paradoxes are expressions of Brahman (the same basic reality).

Thus, this is *ekam*—one entity that is present in all entities of the universe. It is this Self that remains stationary yet moves faster than the mind, like the spontaneous communication between two entangled particles. The phrase 'faster than the mind' is especially significant because nothing is known to travel faster than thought, not even light. In your mind, you take a microsecond to imagine yourself standing close to the Sun but light would take 8 minutes to cover that distance. Your mind and your body, both are you, but while your body stays here your mind can travel anywhere in the infinite universe. However, the Self can travel faster than the mind as well. That takes a while to sink in.

How is it possible for anything to travel faster than the mind? This is where the greatest of all mysteries—

---

[42]Swami Gambhirananda (trans.), *Eight Upanishads: With the Commentary of Shankaracharya*, Advaita Ashrama, 1989, p. 10.

consciousness—comes into the picture. Science is hopeful to find a way to explain consciousness, but as yet it has little to say about it. At the same time, Nobel Laureates like Roger Penrose believe that we could find an explanation for consciousness one day. On the other hand, Vedanta considers consciousness to be an aspect of Brahman, a kind of a reflection of the Self—the ultimate reality. Consider the earlier example again. When you imagine yourself standing close to the Sun, your mind has taken your thought there. However, your mind could logically visualize this scenario only because your consciousness must be there even before your mind or thought could reach there. Hence, the Upanishadic thought 'faster than the mind'. Does it then sound strange when two particles can share information, even when they are billions of light years apart? The answer may or may not lie in consciousness, but the feasibility of the proposition is apparent.

Since the Self moves faster than the mind, none of the senses (sight, speech, smell, etc.) can overtake it. It is thus impossible to perceive it through the senses. 'It being there, allots or supports all activities', is another way of explaining this concept. Since the Self is like space, pervading everything—inside and outside—it is present everywhere already. Space sustains all existence, and all actions take place in space, making it the common thread connecting all existence. Space is of the nature of the Self, hence, a reflection of the same. Because of this, the Self outruns all other entities that try to move. It always reaches the destination before anything.

Another way of saying this could be that all-intelligent entity pervades everything and has no limits to where and how it would communicate.

It is said to remain 'stationary' while outrunning all others. What this means is that the basic nature of Brahman remains constant, unmoving. The basic reality stays the same. However, it appears to be in different forms in different entities. It also appears as varied movement in different entities. Attributes of the entities make them look distinct, yet it is the same basic reality that is expressing itself through all objects and space.

The concept is reiterated in Katha Upanishad: 'While sitting, It travels far away; while sleeping, It goes everywhere. Who but I can know that Deity who is both joyful and joyless?'[43]

Some entity that is so mysterious (and has that much power) is bound to inspire reverence, and hence the word 'deity' comes into the picture. In effect, it is still talking of the same all-pervasive reality. The states of superposition of that one entity being stationary and mobile; in a sleeping state and travelling; being joyful and joyless at the same time—all these opposing states exist as features of that same entity. The words 'who but I can know…' are spoken through the perspective of a person who has an insight into the true nature of reality. In this case, it is Yama, the God of death.

In Adi Shankaracharya's commentary on this verse, it is mentioned: 'Since the Self, as conditioned by various

---

[43]Ibid. 154.

contradictory limiting adjuncts, is possessed of opposite qualities like rest and motion, permanence and impermanence, etc., therefore, It appears variously like a *vishwarupa* or *chintamani*.'[44] The former is a prism, which refracts light and makes it appear in various colours. The latter is considered to be a wish-fulfilling stone that can turn ordinary material into divine things. Thus, reality appears to possess paradoxical traits, which in fact is two aspects of the same thing.

SPOOKY THINGS ALL AROUND

With the progress of quantum mechanics, scientists are able to understand processes that previously seemed mysterious (when approached through classical science). Acceptance of superposition has facilitated this process. As understanding gets deeper, something incredible is being observed: quantum tunnelling and quantum entanglement have been integral parts of our world for an unimaginably long time. These phenomena are happening perpetually. Only, we did not have the ability to identify these earlier. What is more surprising is that these quantum phenomena don't just happen in isolated systems, but also in living cells. As a result, an organism (such as a human being) is a result of zillions of spooky things happening in its cells.

Scientists study quantum features in isolated systems, which are lab-created conditions where environmental

---

[44]Ibid. 155.

disturbances are eliminated or minimized. These are sometimes extremely cold temperatures—nearing absolute zero (perfect stillness that doesn't exist in normal conditions)—or strictly controlled lab conditions where there is no environmental influence. However, the cells of living organisms are like the busiest traffic intersections. Too much is happening within them to describe briefly. And the conditions are warm, crowded and subject to chaotic disturbances from numerous factors. That makes it extremely difficult for scientists to observe how quantum phenomena happen in living organisms.

In the biological world, systems are staggeringly more complex than simple human-made lab set-ups. One of these is the DNA—a complex setup of tightly packed macromolecules that contains the entire encoded information for a particular living being (including blood type, the colour of the hair or vulnerability to certain diseases). The DNA is a double helix made of a sequence of four different types of base pairs, and the two 'ladders' are held together by hydrogen bonds. You could imagine a DNA strand as a spiral staircase, where the railings are analogous to the sugar-phosphate 'backbone' and the steps are formed by triple hydrogen bonds (between the bases cytosine and guanine), and double hydrogen bonds (between adenine and thymine).

DNA is that part of a cell from where biological information is 'copied' and passed on for the formation of the required proteins. This involves making a complementary copy of the information stored in tens of thousands of base pairs, taking it to the manufacturing site in the cell and making an entirely new but exact copy of the original DNA. However, sometimes there is a little tweak or 'error' in copying a tiny part of the information, despite excellent proofreading by the cell processes. This tweak is known as a mutation.

Mutations can be useful in the evolutionary processes. They can be benign (as in minor individual mutations within a cell that can be taken care of in-house) or they can be detrimental (as in causing cancer). Mutations can also be triggered by harmful radiation or in the presence of certain chemicals.

Quantum tunnelling is suspected to play a role in causing mutations—a conclusion drawn from comprehensive research at the micro level in the cells.[45] Since the DNA helix is bound together by hydrogen atoms, proton tunnelling is a possibility. Basically, a hydrogen atom consists of only one proton. If a proton tunnels from one base pair to the other, it causes a genetic change, as the molecular structure is modified. This results in an aberration and a mutation is caused.

On another scale in the human body (and even in other organisms), large molecules called enzymes lend a helping hand in biological processes. Deep inside every cell, chemical reactions need to take place to continue life functions and enzymes help these reactions take place in a faster and more efficient way. Hydrogen ion tunnelling has been found to play

---

[45]Irving, Michael, 'Quantum Tunneling Could Drive Random DNA Mutations, Says New Study', *New Atlas*, 5 May 2022, https://tinyurl.com/3dk4amye. Accessed on 27 September 2023.

a crucial part in this process. Tunnelling helps the molecules surpass the energy barrier and transfer energy quickly. On the other hand, if particles were to be transported, it would not have been an efficient enough process. If tunnelling did not exist, biological processes could not have been fast enough to sustain life.

Apart from this scenario, quantum tunnelling has been found to be vital in the way biological systems get energy. Inside the cells, there are microscopic power houses known as mitochondria. These organelles convert biomass into energy, known as Adenosine Triphosphate (ATP)—the energy currency of living cells. Mitochondria produce ATP by oxidation of carbohydrates and fats. This involves a highly sophisticated and multi-stage process involving electron transfer; hydrogen ion transfer and creating of capacitance; and finally, the transfer of ATP molecules. Tunnelling helps ease the barriers for electron and hydrogen ion transfer, making the process amazingly efficient.

On the scale of large objects, quantum tunnelling at the grandest scale takes place in the Sun. In fact, tunnelling is the primary reason due to which the Sun generates heat and light—the sustaining factors for life on Earth. In comparison to the other stars in our universe, the Sun is smaller and younger. At the same time, at 4.6 billion years old and about 1.4 million km across, it is a gigantic ball of super energy with a core temperature of 15,000 degree Celsius. The Sun couldn't have reached this temperature if it was not for tunnelling. The conditions in the Sun were not originally conducive to starting a fusion reaction in which hydrogen atoms fuse to form helium atoms (releasing energy in the process). Original hydrogen atoms couldn't fuse because the positively charged protons simply bounced off each other. It required extraordinary circumstances to make them override the barrier of repulsion and start fusing. Quantum tunnelling made that happen.

The Sun is only one instance of where quantum tunnelling has been observed. As discussed, photosynthesis allows the energy from the photon to reach the energy centre in a leaf in an unbelievably short amount of time, aided by superposition in various paths. This is also indicative of a tunnelling effect that allows such a high-speed transfer of energy that is not seen in ordinary circumstances—almost an instantaneous transport of the excitons.

Another area in which quantum entanglement is now better understood is migration in the animal kingdom—a phenomena that has overawed humans for a long time. Migration here refers to the seasonal movement of many animals, including birds, in search of better conditions when the weather and food availability in their home gets troublesome. Migration is no small feat. Birds such as the Arctic Tern fly over 30,000 km every year from the Arctic region to the Antarctic region and back—literally from one pole of the Earth to the other. The Bar-tailed Godwit flies for over nine days at a stretch, without stopping anywhere for food or water, and the distance it covers is a whopping 11,000 km or more from Alaska to New Zealand. How the birds have an inherent GPS to reach the same location year after year has remained one of the most perplexing questions.

The most feasible explanation till date has been found in quantum entanglement. Birds find directions by sensing or 'seeing' the Earth's magnetic field. The planet Earth is like a gigantic magnet and has well-defined magnetic field lines from pole-to-pole. The Earth's magnetic field, however, is very weak. According to the quantum explanation, the retina of a bird's eye has a protein molecule called the cryptochrome (which is sensitive to weak magnetic field). This forms a kind of a magnetic compass. When a photon of light strikes the cryptochrome, it disturbs a pair of electrons and one of the electrons moves to another molecule. However, since the two electrons were affected in the same incident, they remain entangled. So, if one is spinning up the other will spin down, and the two are called a radical pair. The angle of the bird to the Earth's magnetic field affects the pair and starts a chemical reaction, sending a signal to the brain. Though many gaps still remain about how the information is carried to the brain, it is evident that two separated electrons communicate information and help the birds see the path to their destination. Many other animals too undertake seasonal migration—sometimes in the ocean (like sea turtles) or on land (like penguins). The remarkable thing is that they never lose their way and reach the same place at the same time every year. That is one truth of nature that needs a massive quantum explanation.

The weirdness of quantum science has a mystical quality

about it. What humans had thought to be true is being challenged. What was thought to be evident has deeper mysteries inside it. The opening of science to wider possibilities has brought it closer to Vedantic ideas—though the methods and the processes of the two disciplines remain distinct. So how do abstract entities—waves and vibrations—give rise to the things we see around us, from the molecules of air, the cells in our body to the giant stars and all of the spooky phenomena happening all around? This is where the most magical and awe-inspiring of all scientific postulates—the cosmic dance—enters the scene.

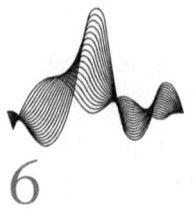

6

Cosmic Vibration Only—*Chitta Spanditam Eva*

'Pratibodha Viditam—It is really known when It is known with each state of consciousness.'[46]

—Kena Upanishad

As we have seen, at the minutest level reality is a host of possibilities—a sea of potential. Just like an electron exists in a mixture of possibilities around the nucleus—existing here, there and everywhere—all particles are subject to numerous possibilities. But how does this operate practically? How can an electron smoothly transform from being a wave to a particle and vice versa? How do electrons tunnel through barriers? This problem confounded scientists

---

[46]Swami Gambhirananda (trans.), *Eight Upanishads: With the Commentary of Shankaracharya*, Advaita Ashrama, 1989.

Cosmic Vibration Only—Chitta Spanditam Eva

for decades, till a whole new approach was proposed. This approach was surreal and even musical in a sense. It is called the string theory.

String theory aims to answer some of the basic questions, such as: what really happens at the deepest level? What is the connection between gravity and the other forces? How does one type of particle change into another and, more interestingly, how do particles come in and out of existence?

This theory proposes a radical, breathtaking idea—that the entire universe is made up not of particles and forces, but of tiny strands of energy called strings. Thus, each 'particle' is not like a point in space, rather it is a one-dimensional dynamic string-like object vibrating in a certain rhythm. The properties of a particular particle, such as mass and charge, are a result of the specific vibration pattern of the strings. These 'filaments of energy' are either open or curved as loops. They suffuse the entire space.

It is the vibrations of these strings and their interactions with the environment that give rise to various particles. The strings would appear as particles when observed on scales larger than the string scale. So, if we could see deep inside subatomic particles the boundaries of the particles would evaporate and we would see fine strands vibrating and dancing to a cosmic tune, and these vibrations create the world that we see. A change in the vibrations of these strings changes the nature of the particle and its environment.

Notably, these strings are not vibrating in random motion. A specific type of particle is the result of finely calibrated vibration of the strings. It is basically the mind-boggling accuracy of these fine-tuned vibrations that create the different types of particles, that constitute this universe. A minor tweak in those vibrations would have implied that the universe would have been something entirely different, and we would never have existed.

Strings are not just confined to particles of matter. One of the vibrational modes of these strings are gravitons—the quantum particle considered to be the carrier of gravitational force. With the explanation of quantum gravity through string theory, science can hope to achieve a unified explanation for all the phenomena in our universe. In the words of Michio Kaku, 'In String theory, all particles are vibrations on a tiny rubber band; physics is the harmonies on the string; chemistry is the melodies we play on vibrating strings; the universe is a symphony of strings, and the "Mind of God" is cosmic music resonating in 11 dimensional hyperspace.'[47]

In other words, it is the vibrations of these tiny strings that is making everything in the universe possible. Strings are at the heart of the fundamental reality. They are omnipresent, irrespective of the type of object or the location in this universe.

Here comes the most astonishing reverberation of science with Vedantic thought. If string theory is the correct description for the entire working of the universe,

---

[47]'Michio Kaku Quotes', *BrainyQuote*, https://tinyurl.com/bdwbnvhp. Accessed on 18 September 2023.

Cosmic Vibration Only—Chitta Spanditam Eva

the following Upanishadic thought is bound to take away one's breath for a moment: 'This duality, possessed of subject and object, is a mere vibration of the consciousness [*Chitta Spanditam Eva*].'[48]

This condensed aphorism embodies a comprehensive explanation of how things come about in the material world. Everything observable or invisible (even what we call empty space), all forms of energy, all the forces of nature, is a result of vibrations of existence—vibrations of the ultimate reality called consciousness by the Vedas. In fact, the string theory perfectly answers questions like why electrons have a mass defined by a particular number, or why another specific number defines the gravitational force on Earth. In all, it explains 20 such basic numbers in physics. It is the extremely sophisticated tuning of the vibrations (or disturbances) on the fabric of primary existence that gives those mathematically perfect attributes to those entities.

To elaborate on the interaction of the vibrations with the environment, the Mandukya Karika explains: 'And consciousness is objectless; hence It is declared to be eternally without relations.'[49]

Existence or consciousness is said to be objectless. In philosophy, an object is something that an entity is aware of and identifies as separate from itself. That creates a relation

---

[48] Swami Gambhirananda (trans.), *Eight Upanishads: With the Commentary of Shankaracharya Vol. II*, Advaita Ashrama, 1992.
[49] Ibid.

between the observer and the object. Existence, however, is Brahman. Since everything is contained in consciousness and is also not separate from it (there is no duality), everything is existence. Hence, when everything is the same entity, what is the question of a relation? How can existence have a purpose other than existence? While unravelling the oneness at the heart of everything, string theory takes us further into the heart of the mysteries of the true nature of reality—in an even more mystical way.

EXTRA DIMENSIONS

Lovers of science fiction hold their breath when extra dimensions are mentioned. These are like the hyperspace mentioned in Michio Kaku's famous statement. The entire idea is so fantastically challenging for the human brain that it takes quite a while to understand how there can be something other than our familiar four dimensions (height, width, depth and time). String theory necessitates the consideration of additional dimensions. For any physical theory, mathematics is the trial by fire. For string theory to make sense mathematically, the usual four dimensions are not sufficient. We need 10 dimensions in space and one dimension of time for the math to work out. Thus, string theory inadvertently introduced the extra dimensions into our familiar world.

Natural questions arise here. Are these extra dimensions just mathematical values or do they exist physically? If they are

Cosmic Vibration Only—Chitta Spanditam Eva

there, why don't we experience them? Quantum physics has the answer to that. We are designed to experience the world only in three spatial and one time dimension. We cannot exist in less than three dimensions. And more than four dimensions are hidden from our view because those dimensions are at such small scales that we cannot perceive them. They are curled up into themselves, or are so compactified, that even if they appear to us we can only see them as one of our four dimensions.

To understand this, a popular analogy is that of an ant on a wire or on a cable. Imagine that we see an ant walking on a cable suspended between two poles from a distance. To us, the ant would seem to be moving in a linear motion. But if we look closer, the cable has a cylindrical form and the ant could go around the cable in many possible ways. From a distance, we might not be able to identify when the ant takes a circular path around the circumference of the cable. Similarly, the extra dimensions could be so small, and snuggled up into compact areas, that our cognitive abilities cannot figure them out. Quite possibly, the extra dimensions are all around us and even within us.

STRANGE COINCIDENCE?

The string theory is the best explanation of the nature of subatomic reality as of now. The theory itself has evolved through different models. One of these earlier variations is called the bosonic string theory, deriving its name from elementary particles called bosons. Bosons were named after the famous Indian physicist Satyendra Nath Bose. This theory proposes the number of extra dimensions as 26, instead of the 10 dimensions in the commonly accepted version of string theory. The number 26 has complex mathematics behind it. Quite surprisingly, it happens to be an extremely strange coincidence that Gaudapada's Vaitathya Prakarna to the Mandukya Upanishad also mentions this: 'Some say that reality is constituted by twenty-five principles, while others speak of twenty-six. Some say that it consists of thirty-one categories, while according to others they are infinite.'[50]

Though it might be too far-fetched to draw a similarity between the 26 dimensions of bosonic string theory and the 26 constituents of reality in the Upanishads, the strange coincidence is mind-boggling. The Upanishadic categories include the fundamental elements, the subtle body, the functions of the mind, the sense abilities and the cognitive abilities (very different from dimensions of space-time). However, what those extra dimensions are for science, is still a matter of research, though the number of possible shapes for the extra dimensions is a mind-boggling 10^{500}.

Could it be possible that the Upanishadic elements that define human existence are manifestations of extra dimensions? Could it be possible that the subtle constituents of human existence somehow work through those 26 dimensions? This is entirely speculative but it is tempting to explore this possibility.

---

[50]Ibid. 247.

Cosmic Vibration Only—Chitta Spanditam Eva

Take for example the sense of smell, part of the *gyanendriyas* or the cognitive abilities. How the human olfactory organ recognizes a particular smell is still a matter of debate. The earlier theory in which odour molecules were supposed to 'dock' into the molecules in the nasal lining for the brain to recognize a particular smell, does not satisfactorily explain the process. A newer approach that considers the vibrations of the molecules to play a decisive part, find more favour with biologists these days. It is proposed that a particular vibrational frequency in the infrared range gives a molecule its smell. So, vibrations are communicating the smell to the brain? But how?

Among the 26 constituents mentioned in the Mandukya Prakarna are included the fine aspects of the human mind, such as *buddhi* (intelligence), *manas* (mind), *ahankara* (ego) and *chitta* (consciousness). Interestingly, in today's world, these aspects are being probed through the lens of neuroscience, but the latter is only a study of the brain and neurological functions. Subtle things like ego and perception are still inexplicable or, at best, they are displayed as biochemical functions of the brain (which again need to be proved). Could the subtle aspects of human existence have an explanation in the extra dimensions? It might be useful to reiterate here that if the extra dimensions exist in our world, they would be so tightly squeezed into tiny spaces that we would still mistake them as one of our regular three spatial dimensions. But this is where the possibility lies: small things are adept at carrying subtle things like elements of consciousness.

It is important to point out that the bosonic string theory has its drawbacks, and has thus been superseded by the commonly known string theory. Yet, this model is still useful in certain calculations. The connections between the two references to number 26 are completely speculative, but one thing is for sure—at the heart of physical world, lies that subtle reality called vibration. No matter which model is deemed more feasible, vibrations of the tiny strings continue to direct a grand cosmic orchestra. It weaves a surreal world where even more magical things are unravelled with time.

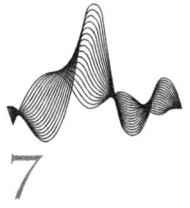

7

The Mysteries of Space and Time

'Concerning matter, we have been all wrong. What we have called matter is energy, whose vibration has been so lowered as to be perceptible to the senses. Matter is spirit reduced to point of visibility. There is no matter.'[51]

—Albert Einstein

We are used to seeing a world full of objects, here on the Earth and far in the sky. A little diving into quantum science tells us that all matter is fundamentally particles, and all particles are fundamentally energy or vibrations. It is energy that is manifesting in different forms, sometimes appearing as particles; sometimes as waves or fields; and at other times as forces and vibrations that

---

[51]'Albert Einstein Quotes', *BrianWeiner.com*, https://tinyurl.com/43xux4uc. Accessed on 18 September 2023.

pervade the entire universe. Einstein's most popular equation, $E = mc^2$ is probably the most well-known scientific image of our times. It also embodies the concept of interchangeability of matter and energy.

Just as we begin to grasp that all matter is fundamentally energy, science delivers this humbling fact: ordinary matter (all that we can see and feel) forms only around a tiny 5 per cent of our universe. The rest consists of mysterious substances. If we overlook all the matter, down to the smallest of entities, most of the universe is empty space. So, what is empty space? Is it a large area filled with air or gases? Is it a vacuum? In common imagery, empty space is visualized analogous to an infinitely large and dark region with no objects, air and light.

Science has come to understand that empty space is not nothing. It is an entity in itself. It has its constituents and its qualities, and it can bend or move. Moreover, space is not something that is out there beyond the Earth. Space is everywhere, even in our bodies. An atom is 99.9 per cent empty space and your body too is 99 per cent empty space.

That is a giant twist in the tale that brings up the obvious question: What is space itself? What is it made of? Since space is everywhere, it has been drawing the attention of scientists and philosophers since ancient times. Till comparatively recently, Isaac Newton's idea of space being a fixed entity was widely accepted. He believed that space was like a stage or a platform, on which events took place. It was as if the various events and phenomena were like actors performing in the arena of space.

The Mysteries of Space and Time

Einstein's ideas of relativity overhauled this notion. Space came to be understood as a dynamic entity that could bend and curve. It was a revolutionary idea. When an object with a large mass (such as the Sun) is placed in space, it causes a curvature in the fabric of space, and objects like the Earth move around the Sun because of being located at a particular position in that curvaceous geometry—much like a marble moving in circular motion on a rubber sheet that has a heavy ball placed at the centre. Thus, the gravity that attracts the Earth to the Sun and the Moon to the Earth is not a force. It is a result of this bending of the fabric of space.

In Vedanta too, space is very much an entity. It is one of the five fundamental elements that build up the universe, including all creatures. The Sanskrit term for it is *akasha*. It is a physical element analogous to, but not the same as, aether in ancient philosophy and science.

The scientific ideas discussed above find resonance in Vedantic philosophy. The first of these is the universality of space. Gaudapada's Alatashanti Prakarna of Mandukya Upanishad mentions: 'All the souls should be known as naturally analogous to space and as eternal. There is no plurality among them anywhere, even by a jot or tittle.'[52]

The implied meaning is that the inherent nature of space inside any entity is the same, be it stars, planets, humans or animals. Since the Upanishads establish the soul as all

---

[52]Swami Gambhirananda (trans.), *Eight Upanishads: With the Commentary of Shankaracharya Vol. II*, Advaita Ashrama, 1992, p. 395.

pervading, and the same in all existence, the analogy of space tells a great deal about what the Vedantic scholars thought about its qualities. They realized that akasha is all pervading, present in all beings and in all parts of the universe. The Aitareya Upanishad mentions that akasha was the first of the gross (equivalent to physical) elements created, when the unmanifested began expressing itself as manifested reality. The other elements—*vayu* (air), *agni* (fire), *jal* (water) and *prithvi* (earth)—came, in due order, after it. If we think of the events at the creation of this universe, the particles that manifested from energy did so in space. Hence, space was there before the other elements could manifest themselves. As mentioned in Y. Keshava Menon's book, 'Akasha is the subtlest of all elements and is filled with an extremely attenuated form of matter. From akasha arises air, from air fire, from fire water, and from water earth. In dissolution, the process is simply reversed.'[53]

The order is not to be taken literally in the modern scientific context. These ideas, presented thousands of years ago, have a different context and translation does not do much justice to the concepts owing to the great gap between the languages and cultures, and the methods of understanding (which are centuries apart). What is noteworthy is that Vedanta recognizes that the gross elements came later than the subtle elements (like mind, ego and intellect) and the

---

[53]Menon, Y.K., *The Mind of Adi Shankaracharya*, Jaico Publishing House, 2015, p. 55.

The Mysteries of Space and Time

unmanifested subtle elements (the *gunas*). Like subtle space gave rise to particles, the subtle elements gave rise to the gross elements.

Another shared idea is that during the dissolution of the universe, the order in which the elements disappear is exactly the opposite of the order in which they were created. The Big Crunch theory proposes the same idea. The larger, more visible entities will go first and the most subtle elements like space will be absorbed towards the end.

Akasha is expressed in various ways throughout the Upanishads. In the Katha Upanishad, the unmanifested form of Brahman is said to be synonymous with akasha. It is said to have the potential likened to that of a seed. Of the five elements, akasha is the highest in the order of subtlety. Again, in the Taittiriya Upanishad, one of the descriptions of Brahman gaining part manifestations, goes like this: 'He becomes that which has akasha (space) as its body or whose body is as subtle as akasha.'[54]

Space, because of its subtle nature, is often used to explain the concept of Brahman. Despite its subtle nature, space has certain mysterious qualities by virtue of which objects of the universe are able to express themselves in it. This makes it all the more mysterious, because space-time must definitely be constituted of something. Space, thus, is not something in which the universe exists, but is itself

---

[54]Swami Gambhirananda (trans.), *Eight Upanishads: With the Commentary of Shankaracharya*, Advaita Ashrama, 1989, p. 269.

one of the constituents that make up the universe. It is a real, physical entity in contrast to being a non-entity. There is an explanation behind it. Akasha is the substratum of sound. Since sound is experienced through it (not to be confused with non-transmission of sound in near-vacuum of outer space), akasha is an entity. Like the other elements, it is created. It appears to be eternal, but is not. In that way, it is not Brahman, though it is part of the same. As mentioned by Swami Vireswarananda, 'The all-pervasiveness and eternity of Akasha are only relatively true; it is created and is an effect of Brahman.'[55] In other words, space supports all the matter in the universe but its own nature remains difficult to comprehend.

Einstein's idea of relativity changed the notion that space exists in isolation from another mysterious thing—time. Thus, space and time—till then considered to be different entities—came to be understood as being integral to each other as one dimension known as space-time. This is also the fourth perceivable dimension of our universe. The fact that the bending of space-time is responsible for gravity, has been validated by precise measurements coming out of real-time experiments carried out over many decades.

Yet, space-time is not a thing or an object. It is not even a platform. It is not like a grid on which different events are placed. Neither is it a vast fabric on which different objects like stars and galaxies appear. To understand what

---

[55]Swami Vireswarananda, *Brahma-Sutras*, Advaita Ashrama, 1982.

The Mysteries of Space and Time

space-time is, our ordinary understanding needs to take a backseat. Here comes the breathtaking idea: space-time is affected by the interactions and causalities of events happening among various entities in the universe. It is like an invisible, undefinable entity that cannot be perceived except in relation to the objects of the universe. And the objects range from quantum particles to huge stars and black holes.

In other words, the fabric of space-time is somehow either caused or brought into notice by the interactions among the objects that seem to be resting in it. Vedantic literature has ample references to the concept of space, time and causation (known as *desha, kala* and *nimitta*). These three co-existing qualities cause things to appear as they are, sometimes projecting an unreal aspect of reality. These three aspects, in coordination, make the universe appear to us in the way we see it.

A new idea in quantum physics, strongly supported by numerous sections of the scientific community, is that space-time probably emerges from quantum entanglement. This means that the mysterious aspects interact in some way to give us an apparent space-time. Could the constituents of space and time be entangled in a way that causes phenomena? Or could it be the other way, something causes space and time to be entangled with each other, presenting the phenomena as we understand them?

THE 'GOD' PARTICLE

As mentioned in the Chandogya Upanishad, 'That which is called Akasha is the revealer of all names and forms. That within which these names and forms are, is Brahman, the immortal, the Self.'[56] The words 'revealer of all names and forms' bear an unmistakable resonance to one of the most important discoveries of the twenty-first century—the God particle. It somewhat accidentally came to be called the 'God particle', but more accurately it is called the Higgs boson (and even more correctly it is called the Higgs field). The Vedantic akasha is itself not perceivable, but hides in it certain attributes that make it possible for things and forces to manifest themselves. The Higgs field is precisely that attribute of space because of which particles and objects in the universe gain identities, because it is the interaction with this field that leads to particles having unique masses. To understand this, a little background is needed.

In the middle of the twentieth century, one of the most nagging questions that physicists were facing was how the particles in the universe get their mass. All fundamental particles have a specific number that denotes their mass. For example, the mass of a proton is 1.67×10^{-27} kg. Roughly speaking, mass is the resistance that a particle will offer when a force is applied on it. In common usage, mass is considered

---

[56]Swami Gambhirananda (trans.), *Eight Upanishads: With the Commentary of Shankaracharya*, Advaita Ashrama, 1989, p. 113.

The Mysteries of Space and Time

the same as weight but the latter is because of the force of gravity that it experiences. If you weigh 70 kg on Earth, you will weigh only one-sixth of that on the Moon because of the lesser gravity over there, but the mass of your body will remain the same. All fundamental particles in the universe have a specific mass. This puzzled scientists because they could not understand what invisible force interacted with the particles even in 'empty' space. It was British physicist Peter Higgs, who came up with a radical proposal.

He theorized that there was a very basic field that infused all of space. This force field, now known as the Higgs field, was that invisible substance that pervaded all of space. Since particles interact with space and in fact, exist in space, all particles acquire mass because of their interaction with this field. This must be the mysterious force that was interacting with the particles to give them their peculiar identities.

It took more than 50 years for the idea of the Higgs field to become an actuality. The discovery was made at the famous Large Hadron Collider, the most powerful particle accelerator in the world, located at CERN (Conseil Européen pour la Recherche Nucléaire).[57] It was a grand moment in the history of scientific quest, and an answer to what invisible substance permeated the entire space-time. Thus, akasha, having the property of being the revealer of all names and forms, is not very different from space that has the Higgs field (responsible

---

[57] 'The Higgs Boson', *CERN*, https://tinyurl.com/2jrjd5rc. Accessed on 27 September 2023.

for all particles having mass). The fundamental particle of this field is called the Higgs boson. It is the only known fundamental particle without a spatial orientation called the spin. In short, this particle is as basic as it can get.

The Higgs field probably came into existence shortly after the Big Bang and gave particles their mass. If the particles had not acquired mass, matter would not have been created, since it would have been impossible for protons and electrons to come together to form the most primary atoms in the universe—the hydrogen atoms. This means that this aspect of space, the Higgs field, was not present as an eternal entity. Once again, this resonates with the Vedantic idea that the akasha was the first element to be created and other elements followed after that.

Swami Vivekananda, one of the most iconic thinkers of Vedanta in modern times, mentioned these ideas in one of his lectures: 'There is the unity of force, Prana, there is the unity of matter, called Akasha.'[58] *Prana* is the omnipresent manifesting force or power. Hence, even in Vedanta, there is one primal force that causes the other forces and elements to manifest.

Swami Vivekananda's *Raja Yoga*, gives a clear picture of akasha: 'It is the omnipresent, all-penetrating existence. Everything that has form, everything that is the result of combination, is evolved out of this Akasha…every form that

---

[58]'The Vedanta', *SwamiVivekananda*, https://tinyurl.com/2k26x7md. Accessed on 18 September 2023.

we see, everything that can be sensed, everything that exists.'[59] He further says, 'At the end of a cycle the energies now displayed in the universe quiet down and become potential. At the beginning of the next cycle they start up, strike upon the Akasha, and out of the Akasha evolve these various forms, and as the Akasha changes, this Prana changes also into all these manifestations of energy.'[60]

Thus, space or akasha is the fundamental, omnipresent entity that moulds how the universe will turn out to be. In his book *Until the End of Time*, physicist Brian Greene explains how the change in the value of the Higgs field would mean that the universe would also change drastically. This universe has a Higgs field with a constant value of 246. It has maintained this constant value since the Big Bang. But if there is even a slight change in this value (and that can happen due to quantum tunnelling), all fundamental particles will change and matter in all forms (as we have now) will disintegrate. Greene says, 'Because the Higgs field redefines what we mean by emptiness—the emptiest of empty space anywhere in the observable universe contains the Higgs field with a value 246—quantum tunnelling of the Higgs field's value reveals an instability of space itself.'[61]

Greene further explains that though quantum tunnelling

---

[59]'Chapter III – Prana', *SwamiVivekananda*, https://tinyurl.com/4uhjshmy. Accessed on 18 September 2023.
[60]Ibid.
[61]Greene, Brian, *Until the End of Time: Mind, Matter, and Our Search for Meaning in an Evolving Universe*, Penguin Books Limited, 2020, p. 296.

of Higgs is a possibility, somehow, it does not happen in our universe. Somehow, the value stays constant. The reason is unknown, but it appears that the Higgs value 'is hemmed in on all sides by formidable barriers: if the Higgs field was to try migrating from 246 to a larger or smaller number, the barrier would forcefully drive it back to its original value'.[62] This formidable barrier ensures that our universe looks and behaves the way it currently does. Particles have their unique mass, elements have their characteristics and forces of nature work to ensure the continuity of the processes.

This thought has an eerie echo in the Katha Upanishad, though not with a word-to-word relevance. The text explains why the forces of the universe act in a way that sustains the world. The text mentions, 'All this universe that there is, emerges and moves because there is the supreme Brahman which is a great terror like an uplifted thunderbolt.'[63] It also mentions, 'From fear of Him fire burns, from fear shines the sun; from fear run Indra and Air, and Death, and the fifth.'[64]

The 'terror' and 'fear' in these verses are in an ancient context, and it would be inappropriate to judge them according to modern understanding. The idea is that it is Brahman, and the entities manifested from it, that ensure that all the fundamental forces and entities of nature behave

---

[62] Ibid.
[63] Swami Gambhirananda (trans.), *Eight Upanishads: With the Commentary of Shankaracharya*, Advaita Ashrama, 1989.
[64] Ibid.

in a way that maintains our universe in its current state. As long as the guiding force does not waver, the values will remain constant. Thus, space-time as we know it, will remain as it is. That brings us to the next mysterious thing in our existence—time.

IS TIME REAL?—IS THE PAST STILL HERE?

Einstein's relativity changed the notion of time, integrating it with space. With Einstein's discoveries, it was also understood that time is not absolute but relative. But what exactly is time? A common understanding of time is what is shown on the clocks and watches. But clocks are merely keeping pace with something. They are not *creating* time. If all the clocks on Earth were stopped, day would still turn into night; days into months; and months into years. Time is not created by a calendar or by periodicity either. If everyone on Earth stops keeping track of seasons and years, babies will still grow into adults and seeds will still germinate to become plants.

More intriguingly, why does time always flow in one direction? Why does our existence always move towards the future and not towards the past? In addition, science wonders if time is a fundamental quality of the universe or is it emergent, and a result of certain events? When it comes to time, all descriptions become abstract and slightly philosophical. Basically, for practical purposes, time is taken as a unit of measurement. In essence, Einstein's equations shattered the idea of time being absolute. In other words, time could have different meanings for each person, depending on how each of us are moving and at what speed.

To understand this, take the famous quantum example of two identical twin brothers, separated at birth. One goes to live on a high mountaintop and the other lives near sea-level. After a few years, it will be found that the one living higher up is ageing faster, though the difference would be so little that it won't be noticeable without scientific interference. This is because the more the effect of gravity the slower time appears to move, as in the case of the brother living at sea-level.

Time is relative according to the frame of reference also. A moving clock will go slower than a clock that remains stationary. One explanation is that space and time mutually adjust in a way that the speed of light remains constant. In layperson's terms, if you are moving faster through space, time will appear to move slowly for you, in comparison to a person who is sitting on Earth, for whom time will appear to move faster. The idea was captured creatively in the 2014 movie *Interstellar*. These ideas seem bizarre and are hard to even imagine, but the relative nature of time has been proved accurately by carefully organized experiments (a number of times since Einstein).

Now, there is ample evidence that time is relative. A modern-day usage of this is the Global Positioning System (GPS) that enables you to find a location using satellite signals on your phone. This extremely high-precision technology needs to be accurate down to nanoseconds, otherwise your GPS would take you to destinations totally off the mark.

The Mysteries of Space and Time

About two dozen satellites, responsible for providing you this facility, are moving at a speed of around 14,000 km per hour in the orbit of the Earth. One second on those satellites is lesser than what one second is on Earth. This is called time dilation. Not only this, to stationary observers on Earth, time on these satellites seems to go faster. This is another feature of relativity. Thus, time has to be 'adjusted' using mathematics for you to get the right location (correct to a few metres) in real time. If the adjustment was not done, the GPS would never have been able to tell you correct location.

Thus, the way each of us experience time might be different. If you could travel at the speed of light, time would seem to stop for you. This has similarities with the way the Bhagavad Gita is said to have been delivered in the battlefield of Mahabharata. The setting was extraordinary. Two armies faced each other on the battlefield, ready to begin the war, when Arjuna (the star warrior) develops self-doubt. At this moment, Krishna delivers layers of knowledge to Arjuna—which, in the form of a book, runs into nothing less than 18 chapters containing 700 verses. Moreover, it is only Arjuna who is the receiver of the knowledge. The others around them have no clue that a lengthy dialogue is going on between Krishna and Arjuna. For the others, this interlude did not happen. Even if the author of the Mahabharata (of which the Bhagavad Gita is a part) had stretched his imagination in documenting this epic, the concept of relativity of time was well understood there. Otherwise, it would have been impossible to incorporate a voluminous and profound discourse in the real-time framework of a few seconds.

Thus, time is understood in relation to other events and phenomena, which makes it even more difficult to explain it in isolation. There is an ongoing debate between physicists who believe that time is *fundamental*, and those who believe that time is *emergent*. For the first, time is just there—it is a basic thing that is a part of our universe. The second argument is that time is nothing but a sequence of events—events that happen in a certain direction in the universe. In quantum physics, space-time is usually taken as a basic reality that is always there. Interestingly, the laws of physics say that it is possible for time to run backwards, and there is a complex explanation behind why this is not happening in the current universe.

If time doesn't sound confusing enough already, there is another aspect of it as well. Quantum physics proposes that the past, present and future all coexist. All three exist in this moment and at all moments. There is a famous letter of Einstein's with profound words on the nature of time. When his close friend Michele Besso died, Einstein wrote a letter of condolence to the family, that contained these words: 'Now he has departed from this strange world a little ahead of me. That means nothing. For us believing physicists the distinction between past, present, and future only has the meaning of an illusion, though a persistent one.'[65]

---

[65] Falk, Dan, 'A Debate over the Physics of Time', *Quantamagazine*, 19 July 2016, https://tinyurl.com/2mryhn8n. Accessed on 27 September 2023.

The Mysteries of Space and Time

THE NATURE OF TIME IN THE UPANISHADS

The concept of time (as mentioned in the Upanishads) is different from the divisions of time described in great detail in later Indic cosmology, where there are precise mathematically calculated divisions into *yugas* (each with its own sub-divisions). In the later texts, time is described as cyclical. That does not unravel the mystery of the basic nature of time. In Vedanta, time is considered more on the level of basic truth. It is closer to the question 'What is time?' Though there are references to *ritus* (seasons) and the cyclic attributes of time, the Upanishads don't dwell on the structural organization of time. References to time are subjective and mentioned contextually throughout the texts. Notably, time is mentioned mostly as being associated with space.

One primary feature is that the Upanishads present the idea that time is not eternal. It is created, and it is created with the purpose of providing some structure to existence. The Agma Prakarna mentions, 'People engrossed in the thought of time (to wit, astrologers) consider that birth of beings is from time.'[66]

The point being stressed here is that whatever is in time, is not the absolute reality. It is merely a projection of the Absolute. Time is not the cause of the manifested world. This is because the ultimate reality, Brahman, is birthless

---

[66]Swami Gambhirananda (trans.), *Eight Upanishads: With the Commentary of Shankaracharya Vol. II*, Advaita Ashrama, 1992.

and timeless. Brahman is thus beyond time. This is reiterated once again in Gaudapada's Alatashanti Prakarna of Mandukya Upanishad, 'Nothing whatsoever is born that already exists, does not exist, or both exists and does not exist.'[67] As also mentioned in the Brihadaranyaka Upanishad, 'The aim of all the Upanishads is to teach about this Self. No one can say at what time ignorance has come upon us, for time is the creation of ignorance.'[68]

Coming once again to the story of Nachiketa in the Katha Upanishad, the little child in conversation with Yama expresses the desire to know a reality that is separate from cause and effect; from the past, future and present. He wants to understand the true nature of reality, that is not limited by the three modes of time—past, present and future. Yama gives him an elaborate and profound explanation of the true nature of reality that is beyond any attributes, beyond time as well. The subjective nature of time is once again presented in the Vaitathya Prakarna by Gaudapada: 'Things that exist internally as long as the thought lasts and things that are externally related to two points of time, are all imaginations. Their distinction is not caused by anything else.'[69]

Here is a thought echoing quantum science: the period between two events in space is time. And if a person sees

---

[67]Ibid.
[68]Swami Jagadiswarananda, *The Brihadaranyaka Upanishad*, Swami Madhavananda (ed.), Sri Ramakrishna Math, 2023, p. 108.
[69]Swami Gambhirananda (trans.), *Eight Upanishads: With the Commentary of Shankaracharya Vol. II*, Advaita Ashrama, 1992.

The Mysteries of Space and Time

events related between two points in time, it is imagination. Time, thus, seems to be unreal—an emergent attribute of space-time.

The Upanishads do not mention time as a fundamental element needed for the creation of the world. The primal manifesting force (prana) creates the Sun and the Moon, keepers of the seasons. And as the Prashna Upanishad points out, prana is born from the Self or Brahman. Hence, time emerges out of certain actions of the vital force. Y. Keshava Menon, in his commentary on the philosophy of Adi Shankaracharya, mentions: 'There cannot be a beginning in time and space for something which is the cause of time and space. Beyond the mind, these problems do not exist at all.'[70]

The trio of desha, kala, nimitta is often mentioned throughout the Upanishadic texts. The interweaving of time and space with the third concept of causality brings us to the breathtakingly sublime concept of Maya.

---

[70]Menon, Y.K., *The Mind of Adi Shankaracharya*, Jaico Publishing House, 2015, p. 62.

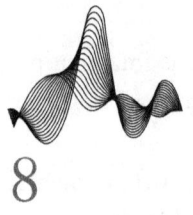

8

Is the Real Unreal?

'Real, yet not real, an illusion, yet not an illusion.'[71]

—Swami Vivekananda

DOES THE OBSERVER CAUSE THE OBSERVATION?

Causality is another addition to the list of seemingly weird things in quantum science. This, along with superposition, entanglement and tunnelling takes the human thought to a place where boundaries between science and magic seem to blur. If it was not for experimentally proved data, time and again, quantum phenomena might have seemed like the fantasy of a crazy mind. But the amazement does not stop here. We know that the phenomena are real, but how do we

---

[71]'Swami Vivekananda's Quotes on Maya', *VivekaVani*, https://tinyurl.com/24mza2xx. Accessed on 27 September 2023.

Is the Real Unreal?

know that we are perceiving the real thing? In other words, despite impressive experimental evidence, science struggles with what is known as the 'observation problem' or the 'quantum measurement problem'.

To put it in simple terms, the problem is something like this. Whenever a measurement or an observation is taken for a quantum process, a definite result is obtained. However, before the measurement is taken, the system is in a superposition of opposite states. For example, an electron exists in a cloud of probability around the nucleus—existing here, there and everywhere at the same time. But when the observation is made, the electron appears definitively at one place. This will always happen, no matter how many times you repeat the process. The probabilities work out perfectly in mathematical calculations, but in a physical observation there is always just one outcome.

So, does the presence of the observer somehow influence the result of the process? Can your brain or your consciousness have a different effect on the electron than my brain? Does consciousness even play a part? Can each of us somehow influence the outcome of the process using our mind? Out of the various probabilities of a system, can we 'choose' (consciously or unconsciously) one result as the outcome? In scientific terms, does the presence of an observer cause a collapse of the wave function?

The puzzle is hard to solve because quantum systems work perfectly when particles are in isolation, but whenever an interaction occurs the wave function collapses and gives one result. The catch is that nothing can be observed without an interaction. There has to be an observer—a person or a device—taking the measurement. Besides, there are continuous interactions with the environment too—with the detector; the display of the detector; the machinery; and even the particles of the observer's brain (who might not be present at the site, but could be there when the observation is read). The dilemma is that to take a measurement an interaction of some kind will always be there.

One of the possible explanations for this is known as the 'many worlds interpretation', first proposed by American physicist Hugh Everett. This theory postulates that the wave function never actually collapses. What really happens is decoherence. The one outcome that we see is true for 'this' world, while all the other possible outcomes will come out true in the 'other worlds'. The drastic idea is that there is one 'universal wave function' that manifests in different forms in different locations. What we observe here is only one of those, but all the others are also true.

Like the other aspects of quantum physics, this also takes a while to sink in. It is bizarre. There has been support for this theory, but also a lot of criticism because it implies that all the possible outcomes of an event *will* happen—and this means that there have to be an unlimited number of universes.

In contrast to this idea, is a postulation by Roger Penrose—one of the greatest minds of our times. He says that a system remains in a state of superposition till a limit is reached, where space-time curvature (responsible for gravity) reaches a certain level. There can be only a certain energy difference between the two states. Thus, large objects (like human beings) cannot exist in a state of superposition for a measurable amount of time but an electron can. This will make anyone's imagination go wild. Does it mean that you or I could have been in a superposition of two states at some time, but the time period was so small that we didn't even notice it? It is almost a necessity that gravity would force such particles to collapse into one state.

String theory, which also includes the possibility of having a multiverse, stresses upon the presence of an observer. It says that if a universe has such properties that it allows for an observer to be present, only then will it be observed. In simpler words, other universes could be hidden from us, but if we could somehow observe them they would become visible.

The 2022 Nobel Prize in physics has brought forth a spectacular discovery that is bound to change the perspective of the world forever. As mentioned earlier in the book, the prize was awarded to three physicists working in the area of quantum entanglement (Alain Aspect, John F. Clauser and Anton Zeilinger). The concept they unearthed has been popularly publicized as 'the universe is not locally real'. What this means is that objects in the universe do not have definite properties till they are observed. It also means that objects can be influenced by something other than their environment, and that information can travel faster than light. That is as 'spooky' as Einstein might have imagined, and it also proved the great scientist wrong in thinking that there could be no instant communication between two particles. It is experimentally established now, after decades of research, that particles may not have definite properties till they are measured. The objective reality might not actually exist. However, this does not imply that there are no laws governing this process. There are rules governing the working of the universe, but those laws haven't been fully understood yet in the light of the newer discoveries.

This brings in the role of consciousness, a topic that unsettles physicists—not because they cannot understand it, but because quantum science is still in too young a stage to experimentally establish the existence of consciousness. The universe not being 'real' locally, could imply that there is a consciousness that is making the universe appear as it is to us. It could be the individual's consciousness or a universal entity that keeps all objects in it entangled. Quantum science could well be moving in the direction where its understanding will agree with the Vedantic understanding, but that will take time.

Meanwhile, the universal consciousness in Vedanta is also the universal observer and is called *sakshi* (the witness). This observer is present in every creature in the form of an aspect of the Absolute. The creatures themselves are oblivious to the presence of this observer within themselves, and the reason is ignorance or avidya. Since they are not aware, the way they perceive the world is through a faulty perspective. This also leads them to focus on causality—the intricacies of cause and effect. Empirically, cause and effect seem to be present. But are they real?

WHAT COMES FIRST—THE CAUSE OR THE EFFECT?

The question seems illogical, almost wrong. In physics, the past and the future are illustrated through the famous image of 'light cones'. They are primarily diagrammatic representations of two cones (shaped like birthday caps) joined at their tips with their bases facing the opposite sides. The point of intersection is the present moment; the area of the cone below it is the past; and the area of the cone above it is the future. Any event that has happened in the past light cone cannot travel to the future, and any event that will happen in the future light cone cannot be pushed to the past light cone, without going through the present. This is an oversimplification of the concept to illustrate that in classical quantum physics the effect is not expected to come before the cause.

However, recent developments in quantum physics have made scientists reconsider if there is a deterministic sequence to cause and effect. One of the reasons for this is the greatly probabilistic nature of quantum physics. Because of superposition, any event is in at least two states of probability before it is observed. Once it is observed, the system collapses into one of the possibilities. This pushes causality into the philosophical domain.

Just like the seemingly paradoxical problem of causality in quantum physics, Vedanta too has a complicated proposition about cause and effect. Different schools of Vedantic philosophy differ in opinion on causality. The most commonly accepted view is that anything that exists must have a cause, because existence cannot come out of nothingness. But whatever can be tagged as having a beginning, is not the absolute reality. Brahman gives rise to everything, yet it is not the cause of the empirical world. The universe is merely an appearance of Brahman. The latter does not cause it per se, yet entities manifested from it are the cause of the material world. They are Brahman in effect. As mentioned in the Alatashanti Prakarna, 'A cause is not born of a beginningless effect; nor does an effect naturally come out of a beginningless cause. Cause and effect are thus birthless, for a thing that has no cause, has certainly no birth.'[72]

The argument is circular and confusing, not just to the layperson but to Vedantic philosophers as well. To get a better understanding, one needs to delve into the most complex problem in science as well as in Vedanta—the observer problem, the question of causality, the illusion of reality or simply *maya*.

THE ILLUSIVE MAYA

In a given system, it is the presence of the observer that brings forth one result out of different possibilities. As we have seen above, the observer does not cause a change to the system (at least not consciously) though the role of consciousness is

---

[72]Swami Gambhirananda (trans.), *Eight Upanishads: With the Commentary of Shankaracharya Vol. II*, Advaita Ashrama, 1992.

Is the Real Unreal?

uncertain and still a matter of study. Yet somehow, it is the presence of the observer (or perhaps the quantum particles of their brain) that makes it appear like the system gave one definite observation. However, the laws of physics stay the same. Do the observers 'imagine' one of the results? Or, as some thinkers had postulated, do things exist because we see them? The latter argument has been refuted many times, because our experiences are empirically real.

An entire Vedantic book from the fourteenth century is devoted to understanding the observer and the observed. It is called *Drig-Drisya-Viveka*, translated as Seer, Seen and Judgement (discrimination or right knowledge). The work is often attributed to Vidyaranya Swami, but also sometimes to Adi Shankaracharya. The book explores in depth, the observer problem. After acknowledging in detail that our experiences are real, the author mentions: 'The existence of the material world is a matter of indubitable experience. The question arises, what is its cause? Brahman, which is beyond all causal relations cannot create it. Therefore, the scriptures postulate maya as the cause of the universe. This maya is extremely illusive. It cannot be described either as real or unreal.'[73]

Here enters the mysterious concept of maya, considered to be the most difficult subject in all of Vedantic philosophy. Maya cannot be said to be real or unreal. It makes us perceive the unreal world as real, it clouds our judgement and works

---

[73]Swami Nikhilananda (trans.), *Drig-Drisya-Viveka: An Inquiry into the Nature of the 'Seer' and the 'Seen'*, Advaita Ashrama Publication Division, 2006.

through avidya. At the same time, it can lead us to the ultimate truth because the way to transcend maya is *through* maya. There are layers to the concept, each intricately connected to the other. The word maya has no exact translation in English—it is an amalgam of various things, the foremost among which is ignorance. The ignorance of the true nature of our existence is due to maya. It is often translated to mean illusion, but that is only partially true and is applicable in certain conditions.

Where does this intriguing entity come from? Is it independent? The answers to these questions are that maya itself is only an aspect of Brahman—a very powerful aspect nonetheless. It has two primary functions. First, it is the creative power of Brahman. Second, it is the power that veils reality.

As the creative power, maya makes this world appear the way we know it empirically. It makes us judge the objects and the phenomena in the world. It makes us see objects with different forms, colours and characteristics. It causes the mind to see the material world—one that can be seen, touched and felt. In this way, it helps in survival. It causes the unmanifested to appear as the manifested. Due to this, maya is sometimes synonymously used with *prakriti* (nature).

Prakriti is the basis of all empirical things, including matter, mind, emotions, senses and other modes of cognition. Interestingly, it is supposed to be a combination of three qualities, known as gunas—*sattva, rajas and tamas*—denoting knowledge, ambition and ignorance, respectively. These are like fundamental operating principles that define the nature of that entity. Sattva is associated with calmness, rajas with passion and tamas with laziness. Maya in the form of prakriti creates appearances, in terms of matter as well as mental states. The three gunas are present in different proportions in all entities, and the particular proportion results in a specific nature of that entity. For instance, if tamas is present in excess in a person, the latter has negative qualities such as hatred, jealously and covetousness. More alarmingly, tamas leads to an egotistical delusion about self-righteousness. Thus, a person in its sway remains in the dark. However, the proportion of the three gunas can be balanced through knowledge. As mentioned in the Bhagavad Gita, 'From sattva is born knowledge (gained through the senses), and from rajas, verily, avarice. From tamas are born inadvertence and delusion, as also ignorance to be sure.'[74]

Just like name and form are two features of maya, the trio of space, time and causation too is an aspect of maya. In contemporary times, Einstein's theory of relativity is an almost direct illustration of this concept. The very position of our planet in the universe is because of the bending of space-time. And what's more, the universe is expanding and there is no absolute position of any object in it (or any possibility of absolute time). For example, if you are standing here on Earth and a friend of yours is far away in the galaxy,

---

[74]Swami Gambhirananda (trans.), *Bhagavad Gita: With the Commentary of Shankaracharya*, Advaita Ashrama Publication Division, 1991.

time would tick differently for both of you. Time seems to be an illusion and, as some people believe, it seems to be a construct of the human mind. Probably, our consciousness makes us think that the gap between events is the flow of time. Vedanta says that the sense of absolute space and time are illusions created by maya.

This brings us to the second role of maya—its power to veil reality. It hides the true nature of reality, like a curtain. The true nature of existence is, in essence, Brahman. Maya makes us believe that the empirical world that we experience is real. If the veil of maya is lifted, the absolute truth is revealed. Because of this property of obscuring reality, maya is also the reason for all duality. It makes the subject appear different from the object; the observer separate from the observation. Superposition, or apparent duality, thus is also a play of maya. Understanding the working of maya also gives us the answer to the observer problem. There is one consciousness pervading every entity in the world, one unified field in terms of science. Hence, the observer is not different from the observation. The apparent duality is unreal. And this is maya.

The question of cause and effect also arises because of this curtailing of reality. Since one absolute reality is the cause of everything, the effect is not different from the cause. But it is maya that makes the two appear different. This is illustrated with effective examples throughout the Upanishads. The seed contains within it the potential form of an entire tree. The two are one, not separate, hence the seed is not the cause of the tree. An infant grows into an adult, and the two are considered the same person. Childhood is not the cause of adulthood. They are two aspects of the same person. It is because of impressions like these that maya conditions our minds to believe in false duality.

As mentioned in the Alatashanti Prakarna, 'As long as there is mental preoccupation with causality, so long does the worldly state continue.'[75] Maya is responsible for us experiencing the world empirically, but the absolute truth is right there (just behind the curtain). This is illustrated through the celebrated example of the earthen pot in Vedantic literature, most notably by Gaudapada in the Mandukya Karika. The example is of a pot made of clay. The reality of the pot is the clay from which it is constructed. If the pot breaks, the clay remains. Conversely, the pot is not the reality of the clay. Clay will still be clay if there is no pot. The pot is analogous to various entities, including humans. The clay and also the space within the pot is Brahman. It is not different from the space outside it, nor is it any different from space anywhere else in the universe. When the pot is destroyed, the space within it still exists. It doesn't merge with the rest of the space because the separation was never there. If one is ignorant of the above facts, one sees the entities as different from each other. This is maya. As mentioned in Alatashanti Prakarna, 'The entities that are born thus are

---

[75]Swami Gambhirananda (trans.), *Eight Upanishads: With the Commentary of Shankaracharya Vol. II*, Advaita Ashrama, 1992.

not born in reality. Their birth is as that of a thing through Maya. And that Maya again has no reality.'[76] Maya is not real because it is only a shadow. Unlike Brahman, it is not real. This mysterious entity works a comprehensive illusory magic, but what is its own reality?

What is maya itself? Maya is difficult to describe, but there is another—perhaps the most famous—example in Vedantic philosophy that gives a fair idea. This is the example of the superimposition of a snake on a rope. If a rope is lying on the ground, and the light is such that the lifeless rope looks like a snake to an observer, the rope gives the illusion of being a snake. It is important to note that for the observer the snake is real, even though momentarily. It cannot be said to not exist. It is real while the illusion lasts. The primary reality, however, is that it is a rope. That is the absolute reality of the object. Maya gave a momentary reality to the snake, and that was true for the moment.

Another example is how the rays of the sun create a mirage in the desert. The mirage is an illusion of water, but it is real for the one seeing it and has a conditional truth. Once the illusion is broken, the mirage disappears and only sand remains. Similarly, maya creates an illusion of this world being real. This illusion has its undeniable truth, but it is not the absolute truth. We do experience this world as real, but when the veil is removed we are able to see the true underlying nature of our existence. Swami Vivekananda had

---

[76]Ibid. 370.

a term for this—dehypnotization. He gave a call to humans to dehypnotize themselves and come out of the illusions created by maya.

IS ALL OF THIS A DREAM OR A HOLOGRAM?

Due to the activities of Maya, the world and everything connected to it appears to be very real. However, the Vedantic philosophers prove through comprehensive and illustrated arguments that this world is as unreal as a dream. The description for this can get complex—dreams themselves are not unreal. The Vedantic scholars do not deny the reality of the dreams, but insist that the dream state is one of the four states of existence. The other ones are the waking state, the deep sleep state and the highest—the state of pure consciousness called *turiya*.

Dreams are real while they last. In relation to our experience of the world, maya projects an unreal picture which we take to be the whole truth (like it happens in a dream). While we are dreaming, we believe whatever we are seeing as factual. There is no doubt about it in the dream state. However, when the person wakes up they know that what appeared so real was just a projection, and not the reality.

As mentioned in the Mandukya Karika, 'As in dream the mind vibrates, as though having dual aspects, so in the waking state the mind vibrates as though with two facets.'[77]

---
[77]Ibid.

Vediquant

The dual states are of the cognizer and the cognized. In other words, just like you watch yourself in your dream, in life your true self watches you believing in the maya of the world. You could be anything in your dream, a robber or an artist, but your true identity does not change despite that dream. Similarly, your true nature (a reflection of Brahman) remains unsullied by the avidya that takes hold of you during this existence. This is also the reason why Brahman forever remains untouched by falsity, and stays in its purest form despite myriad manifestations of it in different objects.

This Vedantic concept of life being like a dream is well known, and often regarded more for its poetic quality. However, strangely, it finds an echo in the latest findings of quantum physics. It started with the study of black holes.

Black holes are superdense regions in space-time with such intense gravitational pull that nothing, not even light, can escape from it. In common terms, whatever falls into the black hole cannot be retrieved or seen. Legendary physicist Stephen Hawking made some revolutionary observations about the quantum physics of the radiation around a black hole, now known as Hawking radiation. But questions remained about the nature of this radiation. The primary question was that if an object falls into a black hole, is the information related to it lost forever?

The idea was carried forward by Nobel laureate Gerard 't Hooft who was the first one to propose that the universe is a holographic projection. The theory was further developed by Leonard Susskind, another towering figure in quantum physics. The basic idea—a quite mind-boggling one—is that though an object falls into the black hole its information remains suspended outside the black hole in its event horizon in an encoded form like a 2D grid. Information, thus, is never lost much like the true nature of an entity is never lost, though in the moment it seems to be lost to maya.

The holographic theory suggests that this universe is a projection of an encoded two-dimensional sheet that somehow wraps around our universe like a gravitational horizon. Just like a hologram printed on a sheet gives rise to a 3D image when light is properly projected onto it, the encoded information on lower dimensions around our universe give rise to this hologram (which we perceive as our universe) along with all the objects in it. Even gravity emerges from this hologram. This is eerily similar to the Vedantic idea that the empirical world is not real, but merely a projection of the real thing. Our world could very well be a projection of something beyond our perception.

In the words of Leonard Susskind, 'The three-dimensional world of ordinary experience—the universe filled with galaxies, stars, planets, houses, boulders, and people—is a hologram, an image of reality coded on a distant two-dimensional surface.'[78] Just like Maya projects the unreal as the real, the

---

[78] Bartlett, Rodney, 'Transforming Holographic-Universe Theory into Vector-Tensor-Scalar Geometry', *ResearchGate*, 20 June 2023, https://tinyurl.com/2eftpktc. Accessed on 27 September 2023.

holographic principle projects encoded information as the discernible world. As mentioned in the Mandukya Karika, 'This world, when ascertained from the standpoint of its essential nature, does not exist as different. Nor does it exist in its own right. Nor do phenomenal things exist as different or non-different from one another or from the Self. This is what knowers of Truth understood.'[79]

To sum up, the boundaries between the observer and the observed; past and future; cause and effect are all probably holographic projections created by maya. None of this is real. Yet, while we live, the reality of this experience cannot be denied. This life is meant to be lived and cherished, but the more desirable thing would be to simultaneously seek the truth that lies beyond it. This world has a fleeting truth, but what lies beyond is the eternal truth. A moment of infinite beauty and indescribable bliss would be when one is able to respect the truth of this existence and also see the ultimate truth beyond all of this.

---

[79]Swami Gambhirananda (trans.), *Eight Upanishads: With the Commentary of Shankaracharya Vol. II*, Advaita Ashrama, 1992.

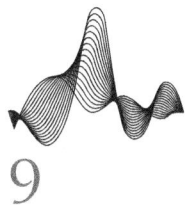

9

Death and Immortality

'In the fullness of time all that lives will die.'[80]

—Brian Greene

Death is the most undeniable fact of life. Where there is life, there will be death. This indisputable fact has been the inspiration for much poetic and philosophical thought as well as a source for pessimism and desperation. Plants, animals, insects, humans—all take birth and all die too. Great civilizations of the Indus Valley and of the Mayans have been wiped off in a flash. Even our Earth and the Moon have limited lives. The great sustainer of life on Earth, the Sun too will die in around 8 billion years, taking the solar system with it. This universe itself will reach an end when nothing will remain.

---

[80]Greene, Brian, *Until the End of Time: Mind, Matter, and Our Search for Meaning in an Evolving Universe*, Penguin Books Limited, 2020, p. 3.

Even time will die.

Yet, the human mind refuses to fully accept this fact—leading to lifelong efforts to attain immortality in one way or the other. Kings and rulers have built monuments and statues in an attempt to transcend immortality. The monuments will crumble. The art will fade. Humans make desperate attempts to leave a mark—through their work, their children, their legacy and such. In short, they try to find any way that will keep them 'alive' longer. 'Leaving behind a mark' is generally treated with respect. Yet, how long will the legacy live? Even that will end. Everything that we observe with our senses will end.

So why is there any life at all?

OF BIRTH, DEATH AND QUANTUM CONSCIOUSNESS

Quantum science and the Upanishads suggest that we have been asking the wrong questions regarding life and death. To see things in the right perspective, there needs to be clarity about the meaning of birth and death; and also, of what lies in between—a sentient being going through life and making choices. The answers that both Vedanta and quantum science provide us are counter-intuitive, nothing like what we experience on an everyday level. But then, how much of our everyday existence do we really understand going solely by our instinct?

Quantum science is increasingly giving evidence that birth and death are just perspectives. Nothing is actually born and nothing really ends. To begin with, take the science behind what we understand as creation (a part of which is the birth of living creatures). The material that formed a living creature, was created out of the primordial particles that were floating around in space. The atoms and the molecules that form our bodies are just recycled matter. The subatomic particles that make up your body and brain, and the subatomic particles of any other living entity on this planet, have all come from that one source which was there at the beginning of this universe. We are all made of stellar material, as Carl Sagan had remarked. Birth is actually just a repurposing of existing material.

Post the formation of an entity, life is a vibrant picture of activity. Its exact opposite is death—that appears to be like a blank canvas. The scientific definition of death is a state in which there is an irreversible cessation of biological functions that sustain a living creature, such as respiration and brain functions. After the end of that entity, the particles that formed the physical body merge back into the environment, entering into their primary nature once again. From that environment are created more forms of life, that grow by consuming food created in the same set up. Birth and death, thus, are simply recycling of existing matter. They appear so momentous to us because years of conditioning have ingrained particular emotional reactions to those events in our minds.

The seat of emotions and feelings is the brain (which dies with the body) but the sentience that differentiates living from non-living is considered to arise from consciousness.

Consciousness remains the 'hard problem' for science and philosophy. It remains mysterious with respect to its nature and functioning. It is widely accepted that consciousness outlives the body. In other words, it is immortal. There are attempts to ascertain if the consciousness of a dead person could be preserved or accessed.

The 2020 OTT series *Upload* is set in the future where dying people can choose to upload their consciousness into a computer system. While their bodies die, their consciousness is given a new virtual body managed by computer programs. After an accident in suspicious circumstances, the protagonist (who has a minor chance of survival) is forced by his girlfriend to have his consciousness uploaded so that the two can stay together. She finances the upload and the maintenance of the upload, and becomes controlling. The series also satirically hints at the corrupt human ecosystem, where even in the virtual afterworld there are 'packages' to choose from depending upon the money a person can spend for their stay and required facilities. It also raises a serious question of the ethical aspect of trapping the consciousness into a virtual body.

Modern science has brought along with it the concept of quantum consciousness. It works on the premise that consciousness could be a result of quantum phenomena like superposition and entanglement in the brain. There are as many critics of this idea as there are proponents. Closely associated with this concept is the theory about something known as 'qualia'. A quale (singular of qualia) can be considered as a basic unit of consciousness. Qualia are responsible for the subjective experience that a person has—an experience that is ingrained in the mind but is hard to explain.

The classical example to understand qualia is that of the colour red. You see the colour red in any object, but can you explain what it is like to see the colour red? The physics of vision can explain why you see the colour. It is because light reflects from the object to your eyes and sends a signal to your brain to decide that it is red. But what if you were asked to explain what is it like to *experience* the colour red? You might recall some emotions, or some comparisons but how would you explain the experience of red and differentiate it from any other colour? That, it is hypothesized, is the work of qualia. Since it is difficult to describe qualia, they are often mentioned as a 'what it is like…' experience. Qualia are responsible for perceiving the redness of the colour red or the painfulness of pain, for example.

Interestingly, leading cognitive scientist and philosopher of the mind Daniel Dennett has listed four characteristics of qualia. According to his definition, qualia are 'ineffable, intrinsic, private and directly or immediately apprehensible' in consciousness.[81]

They are ineffable because the only way to feel them or talk about them is through direct experience. They have intrinsic properties, through which their qualitative character is not influenced by any other event in the brain. Qualia

---

[81] de Léon, David, *The Qualities of Qualia*, Lund University Cognitive Science, 1997.

are private, which means that it is impossible to draw interpersonal comparisons. And here is the most mysterious of these characteristics—qualia can be known directly only in the consciousness of a person. They are, in a way, the properties of a person's experience.

The pure existence of all beings, according to Vedanta, is the witness consciousness called the atman. It is Brahman in essence. This concept is dealt with in depth in the Kena Upanishad. The text begins with the word *keneshitam* meaning 'willed by whom'. The opening verse of the Upanishad has a jaw-dropping similarity to the quest for qualia: 'Willed by whom does the directed mind go towards its object? Being directed by whom does the vital force that precedes all, proceed towards its duty? By whom is this speech willed that people utter? Who is the effulgent being who directs the eyes and the ears?'[82]

Through a series of queries, the Upanishad observes the following about subjective experiences of the consciousness:

> That which speech does not illumine, but which illuminates speech... That which cannot be thought by the mind, but by which, they say, the mind is also able to think... That which is not seen by the eye, but by which the eye is able to see... That which cannot be heard by the ear, but by which the ear is able to

---

[82] Swami Gambhirananda (trans.), *Eight Upanishads: With the Commentary of Shankaracharya*, Advaita Ashrama, 1989, p. 40.

hear... That which none breathes with the breath, but by which breath is in-breathed...[83]

One can explain the process behind the act of vision, but what is vision itself? What is the 'eye of the eye or the ear of the ear', as the Upanishad mentions. The quality of vision is made effective by pure consciousness. It is the same with the other senses as described poetically in the text. There are further descriptions about the nature of the witness consciousness in the Katha Upanishad also: 'This Self cannot be known through much study, nor through the intellect, nor through much hearing. It can be known through the Self alone...'[84]

As with qualia, the Self can be known only through direct experience: 'That which is soundless, touchless, colourless, undiminishing, and also tasteless, eternal, odourless, without beginning, and without end, distinct from Mahat, and ever constant.'[85]

The Sanskrit word *mahat* denotes intelligence. Hence, the experience of consciousness is clearly different from the functions of the brain, such as intelligence and intellect. The description of qualia, as meaning 'what it is like to see red colour' etc., finds resonance in the following: 'What remains

---

[83]Swami Paramananda (trans.), *The Upanishads*, Prakash Books, 2020, pp. 155–56.
[84]Swami Gambhirananda (trans.), *Eight Upanishads: With the Commentary of Shankaracharya*, Advaita Ashrama, 1989, p. 157.
[85]Ibid. 176.

here (unknowable to this self) though which very Self people perceive colour, taste, smell, sound, touch and sexual pleasure? This indeed is that.'[86]

Comprehensive descriptions of the presence and the experience of consciousness are spread throughout the Upanishads, and quantum science is gradually catching up. In a dramatic development, the 'many worlds' interpretation, boosted by recent developments, has given hope to the assumption that if a person is dead in this world they could be living elsewhere, in another universe. It would be too naïve to say that quantum physics has proven that people, through consciousness, are immortal. However, in this theory, even if a person dies in this world, a copy of that person will be alive in another world. There is also a recent concept called quantum immortality. It started with a thought experiment in which the person would theoretically survive death many times, to experience immortality. For a concept such as death, empirical observations cannot show the entire picture—at least not for now. This concept, therefore, remains a matter of continuing study.

THE CHILD WHO QUESTIONED DEATH

Just like the thought of death perplexes people of our times, it similarly affected the Upanishadic scholars thousands of years ago. In their poetic way, the Upanishads explain

---

[86]Ibid. 184.

Death and Immortality

complex concepts through stories. It is important to note that personification of abstract concepts is a feature of these stories and is not to be taken literally.

The story of the little boy Nachiketa in the Katha Upanishad, mentioned earlier in the book, has multi-level expositions as we have seen. The story is even more relevant in understanding the concept of death. Nachiketa observes his father offering gifts after a ritual, as was customary in those times. Troubled by the low quality of the gifts being offered, he assumes that since he is his father's most loved possession he should also be given away so that his father could earn some good karma. The child starts pestering his father, asking who will he be donated to. Irritated, the father replies that he will give him to death.

The words materialize and the child finds himself at the house of Yama. The latter, however, is away for three days and Nachiketa keeps waiting. On returning, Yama feels bad to have kept the child waiting without food and water (since according to the custom of those times, a guest had to be treated with respect). So, he decides to give three boons to Nachiketa. The child chooses the first boon cleverly. He asks that his father should not feel any trace of guilt and should welcome him back home with great love. He thus, asks to be sent back to life. For the second boon, he asks what actions are needed to reach the place called heaven and Yama duly explains the ritual to him.

It is the third boon that Nachiketa asks that puts even Yama in a fix. Nachiketa wants to know what happens to a person after death. Taken aback, Yama exclaims, 'O Nachiketa, do not ask regarding death.' He tries to tempt the child away from the topic by offering him riches and pleasure and other material gifts. But the child is determined, and asserts that all those gifts are perishable. He would rather have something that transcends all of that—the ultimate truth.

After testing the child's determination to understand—for such knowledge cannot be shared with one who is not ready—Yama imparts the supreme knowledge to him. In one word, it is 'Om'. This is a condensed symbol for Brahman—the ever present, unchanging, unborn, immortal reality—the absolute truth of existence. Along with the description, Yama explains that the body appears to die, but the Self or Brahman that lives in all beings is not affected either by death or birth. 'This Self is never born, nor does It die. It did not spring from anything, nor did anything spring from It. This Ancient One is unborn, eternal, everlasting. It is not slain even though the body is slain.'[87]

This Self, living in all beings is so subtle that it cannot be seen easily, but it is not unapproachable either. In individual beings, it is also known as atman. Scientifically, this is the witness consciousness that is beyond the sensory or intellectual experiences of the body. Anyone can sense its presence with the right frame of mind. As mentioned in the Katha Upanishad, 'The Self is first to be realized as existing, and then as It really is. Of these two aspects, the real nature of the Self that has

---

[87]Swami Paramananda (trans.), *The Upanishads*, Prakash Books, 2020, p. 86.

Death and Immortality

been known as merely existing, becomes favourably disposed for self-revelation.'[88]

The text further explains, 'When all the knots of the heart are destroyed, even while a person is alive, then a mortal becomes immortal.'[89] The above verse seems abstract, like all of philosophy does. Yet, on logical analysis the truth shines forth. When a person destroys the illusions of them being the body alone, they realize their true immortal existence. The knots of the heart are ideas arising out of avidya—ideas that one is merely the body and the mind; that one owns or possesses things; that one is happy or sad. The true nature of a person is immortal, and it is beyond all happiness or sadness, suffering or pleasure. It is the unchanging Brahman.

It is that very ignorance or avidya that scientists are trying so hard to transcend. The efforts are in the same direction—to get to know the secrets of the universe that will show us the real picture. In this sense, scientists are the greatest seekers of truth. While consistent efforts go on, some pearls of wisdom are discovered at every step, one of which is immortality. As mentioned in the Advaita Prakarna, 'No individual being, whichsoever, takes birth. It has no source (of birth). This (Brahman) is that highest truth where nothing whatsoever takes birth.'[90]

---

[88] Swami Gambhirananda (trans.), *Eight Upanishads: With the Commentary of Shankaracharya*, Advaita Ashrama, 1989, pp. 227–29.
[89] Ibid.
[90] Ibid. 320.

THAT WHICH IS NEITHER CREATED NOR DESTROYED—IMMORTALITY

The first law of thermodynamics—also known as the law of conservation of energy—one of the things universally memorized by school children, hides within it the greatest secret. It says that energy can neither be created nor destroyed. Quantum thermodynamics has its own version with complicated mathematics involving 'conserved quantities'. The implied meaning is that the total energy in the universe remains constant, even though it can change from one form to another.

There are other conservation laws that describe how a particular measurable property of a system, such as angular momentum, remains constant. Quantum physics has shown us that one type of particle can change into another; atoms can be stripped of electrons; even a proton can be converted into a neutron; and particles can emit photons. This is just like when classical physics demonstrated that thermal energy can change into light, wind and electrical energy. The first bits of matter formed from energy, and the large chunks of matter currently spread out in the universe will ultimately dissipate as energy.

Mandukya Karika reiterates this, 'Everything seems to be born because of the empirical outlook; therefore, there is nothing that is eternal. From the standpoint of Reality, everything is the birthless Self; therefore, there is no such thing as annihilation.'[91]

---

[91]Ibid. 370.

In short, there is no absolute entity in the universe, except the Absolute itself. All the forms, shapes, forces and fields that are parts of this universe are inseparable parts of a single entity. In science, we say that various forces act on particles and fields to form more types of particles and fields. Vedanta says that it is Brahman that manifests into different forms and shapes and energies, through maya. Thus, there is no *actual* creation or dissolution in reality. Reality is like an apparent system in flux, while deep inside it is only the calm, absolute reality—creating ripples on its surface. Alatashanti Prakarna mentions, 'A thing that already exists does not pass into birth; and a thing that does not pre-exist cannot pass into birth.'[92] Vaitathya Prakarna sums it up, 'There is no dissolution, no origination, none in bondage, none striving or aspiring for salvation, and none liberated. This is the highest truth.'[93]

---

[92] Swami Gambhirananda (trans.), *Eight Upanishads: With the Commentary of Shankaracharya Vol. II*, Advaita Ashrama, 1992.
[93] Ibid.

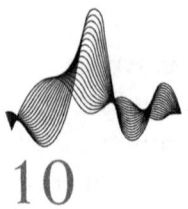

10

Transcending Unknowability

'*Sat Chit Ananda—existence, consciousness, bliss*'[94]

Quantum science is invariably moving in the direction of finding that one unified explanation for everything in the universe—the theory of everything. The Upanishads make a comprehensive, logic-infused attempt to assert that there is only one reality that pervades everything and every aspect of this existence. Whichever of these two paths the seeker chooses, the journey is bound to conclude at the same spot.

Already, the boundaries are blurring. Quantum science asks us to move beyond classical science and to be ready to accept weird ideas. That does not come easy. For the scientifically inclined, it means acceptance of ideas bordering

---

[94]Swami Gambhirananda (trans.), *Eight Upanishads: With the Commentary of Shankaracharya*, Advaita Ashrama, 1989.

on philosophy or metaphysics. But when quantum mechanics presents evidence that the weird ideas, with an undertone of spirituality, are actually the hidden reality of this universe it draws more thinking minds into its folds. Anyone who understands Vedantic ideas wouldn't have difficulty understanding the surreal ideas of quantum mechanics. This is where the stunning state of Vediquant is achieved—a mesmerizing visual of two distinct disciplines pointing to the same truth.

The ancient Upanishads lend a helping hand in painting this Vediquantic picture of reality—they sum up the similarities between quantum science and Vedanta through magnificent and lofty poetic expression. The Upanishads hide within them precious aphorisms that beautifully encapsulate not just Vedantic philosophy, but also the essence of quantum science. The beauty of these aphorisms lies in condensing the deepest of thoughts into a few words. These aphorisms are sometimes just a couple of words long. The ancient Vedantic philosophers probably had no idea that centuries later these expressions would be echoed by quantum science as well. The two travellers thus, can sing the same song and make the journey even more enchanting.

'SATYAM GYANAM ANANTAM BRAHMAN'—TRUTH, KNOWLEDE, INFINITY

'Brahman is truth, knowledge, and infinite.'[95]

—Taittiriya Upanishad

The most famous of these aphoristic expressions are the *Mahavakyas* (The Great Sayings), one of which is 'Satyam, Gyanam, Anantam Brahman'. This one encapsules the entire scientific spirit of modern times. The ultimate secret of the universe is attainable through a quest for truth, an effort to gain the right knowledge and the acceptance that there is something beyond our grasp—that there is infinity. Thus, truth, knowledge and infinity are deep-seated aspects of science as well as Vedanta.

Physicists devote their lives to search for the truth—the ultimate laws that run this world—and each one's effort is a valuable contribution to the pool of human knowledge. The challenges in front of scientists are intimidating because of a factor known as unknowability. This unknowability is an aspect of infinity. Apparently, humans are not designed to know everything, to get a peek into other dimensions or to ever get to see the singularity inside black holes. There are limits to human intelligence, and that is a huge ego-crusher. The fact remains that we cannot instinctively imagine the quantum functioning of our own bodies, but are familiar

---

[95]Ibid. 303.

Transcending Unknowability

with the macro aspect of it. Infinity is beyond our grasp, at least for now, but the acceptance of it removes the ego and adds a subtle charm to our existence.

Despite the enormously intimidating impediments, impressive efforts go on, like the underground Large Hadron Collider (LHC)—27 km in circumference at CERN, working with the partnership of 23 member countries. This extraordinary machine can accelerate particles to 99.9 per cent of the speed of light. Its basic task is to collide particles at that incredible speed, knowing that the collisions will lead to formation of different particles, generating precious information along with it. This information is to be observed by the scientists. The LHC found the Higgs boson and continues to try to solve other mysteries, like that of dark matter. It is one example of the monumental efforts of humankind, efforts to transcend the unknowable, to strive to seek what lies beyond our range of vision and to search for the ultimate truth. That is the path towards truth, knowledge and infinity. Not surprising then, that every day at the LDC is a celebration of the basic oneness of the universe. The CERN Brochure for 2021 mentioned: 'Energy and mass are two sides of the same coin. Mass can transform into energy and vice versa in accordance with Einstein's famous equation ($E = mc^2$). At the LHC this transformation happens at each collision.'[96]

---

[96]'LHC: The Guide', *Education, Communication and Outreach Group, CERN*, September 2021, https://tinyurl.com/59ajxzdm. Accessed on 27 September 2023.

'TAT TVAM ASI'—YOU ARE THAT

'Tat Tvam Asi'[97]

—Chandogya Upanishad

This Mahavakya, well-known and often quoted as 'thou art that', not only carries within it the entire meaning of Vedic teaching but also the essence of all sciences. It is a part of a dialogue between a father and his son Shvetketu, when the latter comes home after 12 years of education. The father asks him whether he has learnt 'that by which we perceive that which cannot be perceived; that by which we know what cannot be known'. When the surprised son says he hasn't, the father explains to him, through the verses of the Chandogya Upanishad, the essence of all being, the true nature of reality and its presence in all of existence. He explains how the essence of everything is that one reality, just like an object made of clay can be understood by understanding the clay (the basic essence). Different objects made of clay, iron, copper, etc., have different forms, but the basic essence remains the same—the material that they are made of. 'Tat tvam asi' stresses on the oneness of all existence, the highest truth to be known. The father says, 'This universe consists of what that finest essence is, it is the real, it is the Self, that thou art, O Shvetketu!'[98]

---

[97]'Fundamental Principles of Vedanta', *Vedanta Society of New York*, https://tinyurl.com/52zutced. Accessed on 27 September 2023.

[98]Swami Gambhirananda (trans.), *Eight Upanishads: With the Commentary of Shankaracharya*, Advaita Ashrama, 1989. .

Transcending Unknowability

The Upanishads, have been asking people to unlearn their understanding of the world, and look at it from an entirely different standpoint. Profound Vedantic works such as Gaudapada's *Karika* make a tremendous effort in this direction. Much like quantum mechanics, Vedanta asks you to look beyond the apparent and to seek the hidden reality. Only, in this case, the lab is one's own mind. Endorsed by scholarly works such as Adi Shankaracharya's *Aparokshanubhuti*, Vedanta asserts that unless the reality is experienced for oneself the meaning wouldn't come across. Understanding is one thing, but feeling it is a different level entirely. Both of these magnificent approaches—science and spiritual philosophy—promise to lead to the secrets of the universe. That would be the destination where the realization of 'Tat tvam asi' dawns upon seeking minds.

'AHAM BRAHMASMI'—I AM BRAHMAN

'Aham Brahmasmi'[99]

—Brihadaranyaka Upanishad

This great aphorism runs the risk of being the most misunderstood. To say that one is Brahman appears to be saying that one is supreme, or any synonymous expression of

---

[99]Swami Jagadiswarananda, *The Brihadaranyaka Upanishad*, Swami Madhavananda (ed.), Sri Ramakrishna Math, 2023, p. 108.

ultimate power. On the surface of it, it gives the impression that one has the capability and the potential of Brahman, thus, one must have that great power too. This is both true and untrue at the same time.

This is most efficiently explained with the example of the ocean—an oft-cited example in Vedanta. The ocean is one body of water; its basic nature is water. There are waves of various kinds on the surface of the ocean; currents of various types at its bottom; bubbles that form and burst; fountains rise up from the movement of the water; and foam too forms on its surface. The foam, the bubbles and the waves appear to have individual identities for a short time, and then fall back into their basic nature—water. This is how every entity is Brahman, apparently different, but the same in essence. It is true that the waves are water, but it is untrue that they are separate from the ocean. Thus, you are Brahman, but the *hiding* of that reality leads to illusions of you being different from Brahman.

Take, for example, this fact: every element in your body, and every atom on the planet, has come from the stars. These could not have been manufactured anywhere else in the universe.

As mentioned by Stephen Hawking, 'We are the product of quantum fluctuations in the very early universe.'[100] The iron in your blood that keeps you alive, the carbon in your

---

[100] Matyszczyk, Chris, 'Stephen Hawking: So Here's How it All Happened without God', *CNET*, 17 April 2013, https://tinyurl.com/3sfzhcb5. Accessed on 18 September 2023.

cells that gives shape to your body, the nitrogen in your tissues without which no growth can take place and the other elements that form every bit of you—all of that is celestial material. And needless to say, any element in your body is the same as in any other human body (or even in the bodies of inanimate objects). There is factually no difference between any two entities in this universe, be it you, your neighbour or the stars. Taittiriya Upanishad mentions eloquently, 'He that is here in the human person, and He that is there in the sun, are one.'[101] Erwin Schrodinger echoed the same idea when he said, 'Quantum physics thus reveals a basic oneness of the universe. Multiplicity is only apparent, in truth, there is only one mind...'[102]

'PRAGYANAM BRAHMAN'—CONSCIOUSNESS IS BRAHMAN

'Pragyanam Brahman'[103]

—Aitareya Upanishad

Many quantum physicists consider consciousness to be an all important entity that holds the secret to the reality of

---

[101] Swami Gambhirananda (trans.), *Eight Upanishads: With the Commentary of Shankaracharya*, Advaita Ashrama, 1989, p. 373.

[102] 'We Are One', *QuantumShorts*, https://tinyurl.com/y2t529nd. Accessed on 18 September 2023.

[103] Swami Gambhirananda (trans.), *Eight Upanishads: With the Commentary of Shankaracharya Vol. II*, Advaita Ashrama, 1992.

the universe. Consciousness, that is the deciding factor of an entity being alive, has presumably come from a common pool. In essence it is no different from the consciousness of any other sentient being, because its basic nature remains unaltered. The idea was heavily endorsed by none other than Erwin Schrodinger and Max Plank, two of the greatest names in quantum physics. As Max Plank wrote, 'I regard consciousness as fundamental. I regard matter as derivative from consciousness. We cannot get behind consciousness. Everything that we talk about, everything that we regard as existing, postulates consciousness.'[104] Erwin Schrodinger thought along the same lines, 'The only possible alternative is simply to keep to the immediate experience that consciousness is a singular of which the plural is unknown; that there is only one thing and that what seems to be a plurality is merely a series of different aspects of this one thing...the Indian Maya.'[105] The ideas of these physicists find Vedantic support in Gaudapada's Alatashanti Prakarna, 'There is no doubt that Consciousness, though one, appears in dream in dual aspects; so also in the waking state, Consciousness, though one, appears to have two aspects.'[106]

This is also the basic idea that all Upanishads explain

---

[104]'Max Planck: "I Regard Consciousness as Fundamental..."', *BigThink*, https://tinyurl.com/4chy3uew. Accessed on 18 September 2023.

[105]'Erwin Schrodinger Quotes', *goodreads*, https://tinyurl.com/2xjpdrpb. Accessed on 18 September 2023.

[106]Swami Gambhirananda (trans.), *Eight Upanishads: With the Commentary of Shankaracharya Vol. II*, Advaita Ashrama, 1992.

assiduously—everything is that one thing. It is repeated as a refrain in the Katha Upanishad: '*Etat vai tat* (This, indeed is that).' It is mentioned in the Isha Upanishad as, '*Soh aham asmi* (I am That).' Again, in the Mandukya Upanishad, the thought is mentioned as '*Ayam atma Brahman* (Atman is Brahman)', meaning that the consciousness in every entity reflects the absolute reality. The importance of one truth is fundamental, but language (a human construct) has its limits. Hence, the unceasing efforts of the Upanishads to explain the reality in different ways, some of which are the great sayings mentioned above.

THE FINAL FRONTIER—THE GIANT HUMAN EGO

One fine day, if you decided to deny the presence of any of your body parts—say your left ear, for instance—would the ear just disappear? However hard you may try to ignore its presence, your ear would be there as a part of you, always. Even if you went to the length of getting it removed surgically, the fact that it was a part of you would remain. The ultimate truth of the universe does not need our permission to exist. It is, and it will be irrespective of our acceptance, denial or manipulation.

'Satyamev Jayate Nanritam' or 'Truth alone wins, and not untruth,' from the Mundaka Upanishad is one of the most powerful statements. It at once establishes the invincibility of truth and demolishes any favouring of untruth.[107]

To borrow the words of Brian Greene to echo the idea: 'Truth in science is not determined by polls or popularity. It is determined by experiments, observations, and evidence.'[108]

Quantum science as well as spiritual philosophy, both have been untiring in presenting extensive evidence of the essential oneness of this world. If all humans are reflections of the same consciousness, why is there so much hatred? Why, despite the best arguments, is one not able to feel empathy towards others? What makes humans violent towards others? What makes them crave authority, supremacy and pride?

There are answers. The universe provides all the answers and they come in different flavours to choose from. You've been journeying through some in this book. The challenge is, how do you react when you see the answers? When you see the truth will you turn your face away and pretend it is not there, or will you allow yourself to move beyond the ego? Would you like to shout down the truth, or would you find a quiet corner in your mind to reflect?

It is ego, *ahankara* in Sanskrit, an aspect of maya, that gives the false impression of differences, and makes you see others as different from yourself. Gaudapada expresses it simply but powerfully: 'Duality ceases to exist after realization.'[109]

---

[107] Ibid.

[108] Greene, Brian, *Until the End of Time: Mind, Matter, and Our Search for Meaning in an Evolving Universe*, Penguin Books Limited, 2020, p. 305.

[109] Swami Gambhirananda (trans.), *Eight Upanishads: With the Commentary of Shankaracharya Vol. II*, Advaita Ashrama, 1992.

Transcending Unknowability

Humans have the most developed brains, the most sophisticated version of sentience and the greatest choices to make. But these privileges come with huge responsibility. Since we wield considerable power on this planet, we are also being constantly tested for the choices we are making. The laws of the universe, like the laws of physics, are infallible. The mathematics is perfect. Every tiny fraction counts. If the progression of our thoughts is towards the truth, as is the case in science, we win. However, if the progression is in the opposite direction—where we are clinging to our illusory world of differences, dominance and superiority—then we are moving 'from death to death'.

'What indeed is here, is there; what is there, is here likewise. He who sees as though there is difference here, goes from death to death.'[110]

—Katha Upanishad

'There can be no perfection for people who have proclivity for multiplicity, tread for ever the path of duality, and talk of plurality. Hence, they are traditionally held to be pitiable.'[111]

—Mandukya Upanishad

---

[110]Swami Gambhirananda (trans.), *Eight Upanishads: With the Commentary of Shankaracharya*, Advaita Ashrama, 1989, p. 190.

[111]Swami Gambhirananda (trans.), *Eight Upanishads: With the Commentary of Shankaracharya Vol. II*, Advaita Ashrama, 1992.

JUST A BLINK OF AN EYE

The opportunity to make the right choices and to seek the right knowledge is the grandest of powers in the universe, much more intense than any power you can imagine. More so, because the duration for which our universe will exist is nothing more than a blink of an eye for the grand progression of the cosmos. Yet, within this miniscule time frame, we have innumerable chances to shape our lives and environments the way we want.

We are like a bubble on the ocean of the cosmos, basking in the momentary beauty of our existence that is extremely fickle. Yet, even in that duration we have a zillion chances to celebrate the truth of our existence. The amazing perception that we have, from recognizing the quantum phenomena that underlie existence to the oneness that is the source and the culmination of everything is extraordinary. That makes us specially placed. It would be a pity to choose the fickle ego over the splendid beauty of the oneness of this existence. Vedanta and quantum science are having conversations along their journey but, quite soon, they might be sitting at the destination, smiling at each other. Einstein expressed the loftiest of human thought when he mentioned, 'A human being is a part of the whole, called by us [sic] "Universe" a part limited in time and space. Our task must be to free ourselves from this prison by widening our circle of compassion to embrace all living creatures and the whole nature in its beauty.'[112]

Kena Upanishad offers the ultimate word of caution, 'If one has realized here, then there is truth; if he has not realized here, then there is greatest destruction. The wise ones, having realized Brahman in all beings, and having turned away from this world, become immortal.'[113]

Both Vedanta and quantum science, ultimately are mesmerized with that one absolute reality appearing in myriad forms, shapes and manifestations. The extremely complex biological processes, the beautiful unfolding of the laws of physics, the mystery of consciousness, unanswered riddles of the cosmos and the inability to describe infinity, add to its exquisiteness. This is the unsurpassable beauty of this existence—the breathtaking diversity manifested from oneness. This could be an illusory existence, but the experience of it is astoundingly profound, and that is what makes it extraordinary beyond imagination.

---

[112]Sullivan, Walter, 'The Einstein Papers. A Man of Many Parts', *The New York Times*, 29 March 1972, https://tinyurl.com/4n7exefn. Accessed on 18 September 2023.
[113]Swami Gambhirananda (trans.), *Eight Upanishads: With the Commentary of Shankaracharya*, Advaita Ashrama, 1989, p. 71.

Acknowledgements

First of all, my gratitude to life, for making me experience grief and sadness that set off my quest for answers to existence, and hence paved the way to bliss and peace.

To certain mysterious, perplexing events throughout my life, that led me to extraordinary experiences, and somehow guided me to the most pertinent sources and people.

To the numerous wonderful teachers in different parts of our world who didn't hold back the knowledge that they have, and to technology that helped me learn from those teachers.

To my kids, Ananya and Anvesha, for their valuable counterarguments. To Amit, for everything.

To all the people who touched my life in various ways, ushering a new understanding each time—especially to the people who triggered negative emotions in me, and hence boosted that learning manifold.

Thanks to the entire team of Rupa Publications.

My sincere thanks to my editor, Dibakar Ghosh, for giving a shape to this entire journey by planting the seed of this book in my mind; for believing in the concept and leading it to this wonderful outcome. My thanks to Sagareeka Pradhan, for meticulously copy-editing the book.

And eternally, my reverential gratitude to the working of existence—that we know by different names and perceive as this Universe and its mysteries.

www.ingramcontent.com/pod-product-compliance
Lightning Source LLC
Chambersburg PA
CBHW032049150426
43194CB00006B/470